# THE GREEN YEARS

# The Green Years

MOLLIE HARRIS

LONDON

ROBERT HALE LIMITED

© *Mollie Harris 1976*

*First published in Great Britain 1976*

ISBN 0 7091 5715 0

Robert Hale Limited
Clerkenwell House
Clerkenwell Green
London EC1R 0HT

PRINTED IN GREAT BRITAIN BY
CLARKE, DOBLE & BRENDON LTD.
PLYMOUTH

# Contents

# Illustrations

# Introduction

*The Green Years* is really a continuation of my first book *A Kind of Magic*, because it is all about Ducklington and the surrounding villages. For after the publication of *A Kind of Magic* I realized that there was much more to tell of my village and the people that my family knew at the time when we all lived, and indeed grew up there. Village characters, school friends, and neighbours. But more especially, the folk we called Aunts and Uncles; some, of course were relatives, others were just very good friends of our parents.

So I have gathered them all up, like a bunch of flowers; some were bright and gaudy, some pale and gentle. In their prime they did their part, sharing and loving, helping and giving. Now many of them have gone down the long, dusty road of memory, and the world is a poorer place for it.

# Ducklington

To Ducklington, the signpost read
And that's the way for me I said
For that, I thought, must surely be
A pleasant kind of place to see,
Where downy and delightful things
With yellow feet and cherubs' wings
And busy bills, and bobbing heads
Will dip and dive in osier beds,
Or dabble by the brooklet edge
And hunt for tadpoles in the sedge,
Or heedless of the careful clucks
Of such poor 'hens' as mother ducks
Put out, true infant 'Drakes', to sea,
On the broad ponds immensity.

Alas the dream, the year was old,
The rickyards brimmed with Autumn's gold
Low bowed the weighted fruit tree's down
The green was parched and bare and brown
And all the ducks that quacked beside
The pond, that drought had all but dried,
Were old and sober, staid and sage
Forgetful in their riper age
That they, in some sweet April gone
Were ducklings once in Ducklington.

But time will come and time will go
And this year follow last year's snow,

And spring come back to Windrush side
With swallows flight and mating tide,
With fleeting sun and flying shower
The coltsfoot and the cuckoo flower
With bloom in spate on orchard trees
And faint frail scent of primroses
And running brooks, and ponds abrim
Where downy ducks shall dive and swim
As broods like them since time began
And grass grew green and water ran
From year to year have surely done
At duckling time in Ducklington.

by C.F.S.
Reproduced by permission of *Punch*

# Acknowledgements

In writing this second book about Ducklington, I would like to thank my brothers and sister, cousin Harry, Mr R. Beckinsale and Mr H. Wheeler, and many others, who, from conversations, have helped to make *The Green Years* a colourful portrayal of village life in the 1920s and '30s. My thanks also to Mary Hathaway, my Mother's friend, for kindly sending the copy of the poem *Ducklington* to me.

Some of the characters' anecdotes have been broadcast on the B.B.C. *Countryside* programmes.

*To my brothers and sisters . . . the whole and the half*

# 1

# Come Summer

"Come summer," our Mother said, "I'll get Uncle Ted Midwinter to drive us over to see Auntie Maggie and Uncle Amos." They lived in a farm cottage away in a field about twenty miles from us, and as no trains went anywhere near the hamlet where they lived, we had to rely on Uncle Ted Midwinter to take us.

We children looked forward to the long-promised trip to Robinsgrove, counting the days, almost the hours, till it seemed that the magical day would never come. Then suddenly, one misty June morning, Uncle Ted Midwinter was outside our gate with his pony and trap. He smelt strongly of polish and horses, his smart brown gaiters and boots shone like glass bottles, and on his thin, wiry frame hung a peat-smelling tweed coat. The trap too was polished to perfection and its yellow painted wheels looked for all the world like giant sunflowers. Pete the pony must have been brushed for hours, for his chestnut coat gleamed healthy and shiny.

We were wildly excited about the journey and rushed in and out of the cottage urging our Mother to hurry.

"It's no good you tryin' to rush me," she shouted, "I shall be all the longer if you keeps on." And she calmly went about her preparations for the journey, stowing away a loaf of bread and a pot of jam for us to eat on the way, and a jar of her apple chutney for Auntie Maggie into a rush basket. "And don't you dare get dirty," she yelled to us, as we kicked dust and pebbles in the garden while we waited impatiently for her. The night before we had all been scrubbed clean in the old tin bath, and changed our clothes, like we usually did on Saturday nights; we had no such thing as Sunday best clothes, but just clean ones each week.

After a while we piled into the trap, Uncle Ted Midwinter sitting up front one side and our Mother the other for balance, and we kids behind.

"Ready then?" Uncle Ted said. Then with the flick of his whip and a click of his tongue we were off through the deep Oxfordshire countryside.

"My goodness," our Mother cried, turning round and eyeing us, "you all looks that clean and tidy, I wonder how long it'll last. She too looked fresh and pink in her print cotton frock; she had picked a small posy of bright blue cornflowers from our garden and had pinned them to the brim of her old straw hat, and I thought that she looked quite lovely.

The first hour of the journey passed quickly. It was still early for we had set out just after six o'clock, and the morning mist hung over the valleys like drifts of cotton wool. Then suddenly it gave way to brilliant sunshine.

"Goin' to be a sweater," Uncle Ted remarked as we jogged along. The verge sides were banked with summer flowers and grasses and the air was filled with the sharp tangy smell of elderflowers.

"Ah," our Mother said, when Uncle Ted remarked on their profusion. "Do you know what my old Dad used to say about 'um? He said that summer was never fully established till the elderflower was in bloom, and that it ended when the berries was ripe."

We waved excitedly to old Charley the roadman, he was just putting his trike in the shade before starting his day's work.

Just after we left the village of Westford we pulled up at the edge of a small wood. We were all frantic to go to the lavatory and squittered off to find a convenient bush.

"If a beans a bean, wass a pea?" one of my brothers called.

"A relief," giggled the other one.

"You 'ent 'alf awful," Betty said, "our Mum 'ud clout you if she heard you say that!"

We ran back to find our Mother getting the food ready. A feast of doorsteps followed. "Doorsteps" we called the thick hunks of bread that she hacked off the loaf, hugging it to her chest as she clumsily cut the bread. "Never a sharp knife in our house," she cried, excusing herself for the thickness of the slices.

Uncle Ted had wandered off to a nearby cottage to get water for us and the pony, then he returned to eat his own neatly cut sandwiches. "We shall be thur be half-past 'leven I reckon," he said, as we all climbed back into the trap.

Three of Auntie Maggie's children were waiting for us at the top of the lane. Our Mother got down and walked up to the cottage while the children climbed into the trap with us.

Auntie Maggie was massive, she was over seventeen stone, red-faced and jolly. Uncle Amos was just the reverse, tall and as thin as a whipstick, and very quiet. Still his wife made up for that, she was always chattering and laughing: "'erd laugh tu see a puddin' crawl" was one of her husband's expressions of his buxom wife. She was sitting in the warm kitchen waiting for us; she was so big that she completely filled the chair, in fact some of her fat body hung over the sides. She flung back her head and laughed as we entered, her numerous chins wobbling pink and wrinkled. Her legs, like huge cider bottles, were wide apart, revealing a great expanse of bare leg and pink stockinet bloomers.

"My blessed Kate" she said to our Mother, "I should think that you was up before the crow piddled this morning wasn't you?" And they laughed, glad to see each other again.

Leaving the grown-ups to chatter, we children all went outside and played for a while, charging round the cottage like mad things; then we shut the boys in the pigsty and when they got out they chased us down to the field pond where we all played ducks and drakes with flat stones. Then young Ernie fell in and we dragged him out—covered in green slime and water weed he was. He went crying back to the cottage. Auntie Maggie stripped off his clothes.

B

"I shall have to wash 'um straight away," she cried. "He got no more tu wear, good job 'tis a fine day, they'll soon dry," and she had them washed and out on the line in no time, while Ernie was packed off to bed where he had to stay till his clothes were fit to wear again.

We all sat round the big table for dinner, eight of them and six of us. We had oxtail stew, thick and lovely and swimming with onions, carrots and haricot beans, which Auntie Maggie doled out from the biggest saucepan I'd ever seen. Afterwards she fetched two piping hot gooseberry tarts from the oven and from the back kitchen she brought a huge jug of runny custard made from milk that Uncle Amos had brought from the farm where he worked as a cowman.

As she collected the piles of dirty plates, Auntie Maggie chanted good-humouredly:

Thank the Lord for what I've had
If 'twas more I should be glad,
But as the times they be so bad
I thanks the Lord for what I've had.

"Go on, outside, all the lot of you," she cried, "while we gets on with the washing up," and we staggered out to the field and lay fattening, like pigs, in the cool grass.

After a while, one of the boys said, "Let's go and play on the trucks," so we trailed off to the edge of a wood where, during the week, gangs of workmen cut down some of the great oak trees and loaded them onto the trucks on the small-gauge railway. The engine pulled them along from the wood to the roadway where they were re-loaded onto horse-drawn waggons. The track ran through four of the farmer's fields, so each time the train went along, the gates had to be opened and shut, so that the cattle did not get out. But on Saturday afternoons and Sundays the little engine was silent, so that it was quite safe for us to play on the track. Auntie Maggie had asked us to pick up some wood chips, which burned well in her big grate, and we all worked quickly to fill the hessian sack that we had brought with us. Then we clambered onto one of the trucks while the boys tried hard to push it up a small incline, but the truck was too heavy for them so we girls got down and helped them and we gradually moved it back up the hill, then we all climbed on and had a ride as the truck slipped back down. But I soon got tired of this and said that I wanted to ride both up and down, so they gave in and said that I could sit on the front. It was fun for a while and then a sudden burst of energy sent the truck over the ridge. It careered helter skelter down the other side and crashed into a closed farm gate. I was knocked clean off my perch, my face smashing into the spars, the truck continued madly on for a hundred yards or more. The boys ran and picked me up, blood was streaming from my nose, my sister Betty rushed up to my side, up went her frock as she swiftly ripped off the bottom of her white cotton petticoat to hold my nose, then she shouted to the others to grab handfuls of cool grass which she stuffed down the back of my neck to try and stop the bleeding.

Back in the cottage I sat on Auntie Maggie's lap while she washed away the blood, my nose was throbbing and swollen. " 'Er'll have two black eyes be morning, I'll be bound," she cried, and my brothers began singing:

> Two black eyes and a broken nose
> And a little bit off of her topknot.

That set me off crying again. "Don't you take no notice of um, my lamb," she said, "you stop your crying and I'll let you swill out a jam-jar."

The swillings of a jam-jar were indeed a great treat. Auntie Maggie had left a bit of jam in the bottom too. I filled the jar full of water swishing it round to get all the jam off. The others stood and watched me enviously as I sipped my lovely drink, but there was none for them; anyhow they had not hurt themselves. Then I nestled down against Auntie Maggie's ample bosom, her huge pink arms enveloped me and I wished that I could stay there for ever pillowed in her warm, comfortable embrace.

Then Uncle Amos came home from work smelling of cows and hay. He tweaked my ear as he passed, "Hey, can you do this?" he said, trying to cheer me up, and keeping his outstretched arm stiff he swung the can full of milk that he had brought, round and round like a great wheel, without spilling a drop.

"Don't you be so daft," his wife cried, " 'er'll be tryin' to do that when her Mother sends her for the milk and you know where it'll end up, don't you?" She went on, "when you've had a cup of tea take her to see Daisy's new calf, that'll cheer her up no end," and I did not give him a minute's peace until he took me up to the farm.

The calf had been parted from its mother and was shut in a small pen, and it looked at us with its huge sorrowful eyes.

"Put your fingers in its mouth," Uncle Amos said; the calf sucked away at my fingers, it had such a rough tongue too.

"What shall we call her?" Uncle Amos asked.

I thought for a few moments. "What about Alice?" I said, thinking of the girl next door.

"That'll do fine," Uncle Amos said. "We'll call her Alice then."

When we got back our Mother and Auntie Maggie had got the tea ready; there was a mountain of new bread, cut thick and spread with home-cured lard, and flycake, as Auntie Maggie called it. It was what we called "seedy cake", but then our Mother explained that Auntie Maggie came from a different county from us, where they had different names for many things.

Soon it was time to go home. Our Mother collected up some flower plants, a new pattern for boys' trousers, and Auntie Maggie's own recipe for oxtail stew.

We clambered back into the trap. "Try and come again next year," Auntie Maggie called, " 'tis bin lovely to see you again," she said as we turned into the lane.

It was a much quieter journey than the outward one had been and we were all sleepily tired. My nose had a distinct bump on it, which I have to this day. Our Mother was not sure if it was broken or not, and I cuddled up to her for comfort. She sang softly to us most of the way home, but the only thing I can recall is:

> The day is done
> O God the son
> Look down upon
> Thy little one

And that was because I thought she was singing it specially for me.

Uncle Ted pulled up outside our cottage, we got down from the trap, stretching our stiff limbs and yawning loudly.

"Shan't want much rocking tonight," our Mother called to a neighbour, and the cat rubbed itself round our legs, welcoming us home.

"Go on, hop off to bed all of you," our Mother cried. "I'll come and kiss you goodnight when I've made some cocoa." But the day had been long and exciting and we tumbled quietly into bed. I remember starting to say my prayers, "Gentle Jesus meek and mild . . ." that is all.

# 2

# *Cotswold Days*

Sometime after our Father had died, our Mother married again. Our step-father was a handsome, hard-working fellow, who had been a despatch rider during the war and at sometime had emigrated to Canada, but then settled down with us at Ducklington.

Our Mother was very keen to show him off to her ageing parents and to her brother and his wife and family, who all lived in the village of Sherbourne in the Cotswolds, about sixteen miles away.

So, with our step-father driving this time instead of Mr Midwinter, we set out in his pony and trap that he had kindly lent to us. There was our Mother, step-father, Bern, Bunt, Betty and me.

It was summer time and, as we bowled along the roads, we met other folk also travelling in traps, waggons and carts, all of course were horsedrawn.

Our step-father, a jolly, laughing man, sang most of the time, wartime songs like "Take me back to dear old Blighty" and "Mademoiselle from Armentieres" with we children joining in, not singing the right words—"Inky Pinky Parlez Vous, Charlie Chaplin's got the 'flu, Inky Pinky Parlez Vous" we bellowed, thinking that we were ever so clever to be able to sing some French words. Along the Cheltenham Road, some way from Burford, we came to The New Inn pub. It was to this same pub years before that my grandfather used to walk every Friday night from the lodge where they lived a couple of miles away, to have a weekly pint of beer, always taken in half pints so that it would last all evening. He looked forward to this outing, the only one he had apart from a day off once a year to go to Stow on the Wold sheep fair. At the pub he met a few of the village men and picked up the local gossip and news.

One hot summer evening he arrived at the inn. There were two or three of his old cronies there and a couple of strangers. My Gramp went up to the bar and called for his first half pint. He put his hard-earned florin down, then turned round to say "How be 'e?" to Fred Ashcomb.

"That'll be one penny then, Joe," the innkeeper said.

"But I put me money on the counter," my Grandfather replied bewildered. But there was no sign of the precious florin. Nobody would own up as to who had taken it. My Gramp turned on his heel, walked out of the inn and never went in one again.

Anyhow, our step-father tied the pony up under a tree and went inside the pub for a drink. We sat out in the trap and drank ginger beer that our Mother had made from a ginger-beer plant that she kept in a jam-jar on the window sill at home. The liquid had to be fed every day with a teaspoon of sugar and one of ground ginger. If you forgot for one day the plant died, and then it meant that you had to start all over again. And our Mother was always letting hers die. Then she would shout, "Go, on, take a jam-jar and call at Mrs Tremlins and ask her if she has got a ginger-beer plant that she could let me have." And Betty and I would go squittering off down the village to Tremlins' house and make our request to the old lady.

"What?" she would cry. "I never see such a person as your mother for letting her ginger beer plants die, I gave her one only last week. And tell her to look after it proper this time," she called to us as we slunk back up her garden path.

But sometimes she did remember to feed the demanding plant and then she made the most lovely drink from it. It was sweet and strong and fizzy, and once one of the full bottles exploded in our kitchen, shooting glass and ginger beer all over the place.

Our step-father came out of the inn, smacking his lips and wiping his mouth; he had enjoyed his pint—all that he could really afford with his ready-made family to keep.

We set off again arriving at our grandparents home about midday. They lived at one of the lodge cottages at the entrance to Sherbourne House and park. The cottages were situated on the main road, but the great house was down an avenue of trees.

Our Gran had prepared a meal for us, lovely rabbit pie it was, but I cannot remember what vegetables we had. For pudding there was a huge dish of lovely red plums and a jug of custard.

We piled into the trap again and made the short journey down into the village to the house of our Mother's brother Uncle Will, his wife Auntie Sarah and their three children, cousins Will, Arnold and Mabel. The boys were busy cleaning out the cowshed and Mabel, the youngest, was helping her mother in the small dairy.

We all settled in the living-room, chattering nineteen to the dozen, then I realized that our Mother was talking about me.

"The trouble is," she went on, "I suppose we all spoilt her a bit, her being the youngest and the fact that she never even saw her father," (He died two months before I was born.)

"Ah, I expect she's had her nose put out of joint a bit lately," my Auntie said, looking at our step-father. "You let her stay here a bit Kitty, a change might do the little maid a bit of good."

Instead of feeling happy at the thought of staying at their little farm for a few weeks, I felt jealous and angry, that was my trouble, I was jealous of our laughing, jolly step-father, and my parents thought that a short break away from the family might cure me.

I watched them go trotting off down the dusty road, they all waved goodbye and our Mother called "Now you just be a good girl and we will come back for you very soon."

Once they were out of sight I stormed and raged and then shut myself in the lavatory down the bottom of the garden and refused to come out. I whiled away the time by looking at a seed book that was hung up behind the door, then I killed several blue bottles that came buzzing in on that hot, sultry afternoon. After a while my cousin Mabel, who was about four years older than I, came to see if she could entice me out.

"Come on," she cried, "come out and I'll take you for a walk, I know a secret way to reach the old windmill. We won't let on to nobody where we are going," she said.

I had never even heard of a windmill, let alone seen one. The offer sounded so tempting and I eagerly left my sanctuary.

She took my hand and we walked over hundreds and hundreds of fields, at least it seemed like hundreds to me. But the windmill, standing up there on the skyline seemed further away than ever.

"How much further?" I cried.

"We shall soon be there," my cousin said.

But I was hot and tired and I sat down in the middle of a field and bawled my head off. I took off my boots, threw my bunch of wild flowers away and refused to walk another step.

We were lost and nobody would ever find us. My cousin sat down beside me, she was crying quietly, wiping her hot, streaming face on her white lace-edged petticoat.

Suddenly we heard voices shouting our names urgently, there were men running across the fields towards us. It was my uncle and cousins who had been searching for us for hours.

"Thank God you're safe," I heard Uncle Will cry as he gathered me up in his hot, sweaty, sunburnt arms.

We had walked over six miles across those fields, crossing Sherbourne brook over a narrow footbridge, we had been gone five hours and we still had not reached the windmill.

Later that night as I lay in the coolest, nicest, lavender smelling sheets that I had ever slept in, my cousin whispered, "Never mind, you and I will go to the windmill one day, when you are bigger," but we never did make it. I walked with my cousins backwards and forward, to and from the village school and hated it and was a naughty, disobedient girl.

One day, after school I was running back up the tree-lined road, crying as usual, when I saw someone coming towards me on a pushbike. In a moment I was in my Mother's arms, being smothered with kisses and hugged very tightly. She had borrowed a pushbike and then she had cycled from Ducklington to fetch me home.

I remember the long, uncomfortable ride home on the hard metal carrier on the back of the bicycle, but at least I was going home.

There was a wonderful surprise waiting for me when I got there. In my absence my Mother had produced a new baby, my step-sister Kathleen (Mick), a fat, curly-headed bundle that looked more like a doll. Suddenly my jealousy disappeared. I was a big girl now, I had been miles and miles away from home for almost a year and I felt quite grown-up.

But from then on, until I left school, I continued to go to stay at my Auntie Sarah and Uncle Will's home for my summer holidays. No other members of the family ever stayed for weeks as I did.

And gradually, over the years, the form of transport that took me to that lovely Cotswold village changed. First of all, I travelled several times in the carrier's cart, then in Mr Midwinter's pony and trap. But the last few years I travelled in a grocery van. It happened that a Mr and Mrs Caswell and their family came to live next door to us at Ducklington in the little thatched cottage at the end of the row. Mr Caswell was employed by a wholesale grocer in the town, where it was his job to drive his van round to many of the small villages within forty miles radius of the town delivering groceries to the shops. And every fortnight his journey took him to Taylor's shop in Sherbourne. So without his firm knowing anything about it, Mr Caswell used to take me there, drop me at Taylor's shop down the bottom end of the village, then I used to walk to my Auntie's cottage up at the top end of Sherbourne. Sometimes I stopped for a fortnight, sometimes for a month. On the return journey Mr Caswell would pick me up at my Auntie's because he could never be quite sure just what time he would get to the shop. Years and years later, during the Second World War, I worked for the same wholesalers and drove a three-ton van all around those same country villages, delivering two hundredweight sacks of sugar, one-and-a-half hundredweight sacks of flour, great double cheeses in crates, and great heavy boxes and cartons filled with goods that wholesale grocers sell.

I even called regularly at Tayor's shop and Post Office at Sherbourne, where we would somtimes reminisce about the days when I went there with Mr Caswell. A snotty-nosed, tousle headed, wild thing, someone said I was, but with very winning ways.

Apart from once when Bern took me on the back of his motorbike, the last few journeys that I made to Sherbourne were made in a very different way than in those early days. In the late 1920s, I think it was, the Black and White coaches began to run from Oxford to Cheltenham. The coach used to drop me on the top road and I would walk down the long, narrow lane which lead to the village, skirting the great Cotswold stone wall which surrounded Sherbourne House and park, which at that time was still the home of Lord Sherbourne. Now the great house is a boys' school, my Auntie and Uncle are long since dead and my cousins scattered. But the tree-lined road through the village is still reasonably quiet and the clear waters of Sherbourne brook flow on swiftly and silently to join my beloved river Windrush.

# 3

## *Wireless Sets and Home-Made Wine*

During the early '20s, only a few families in the village owned a crystal set: we were one of these because our step-father was clever with his hands and had made one. He had bought copper wire, ebonite, and a magic thing, a crystal in a glass tube, which, I believe was called a "cat's whisker", because of its fineness. This cat's whisker had to be twiddled very carefully so that it contacted some other part of the wonderful contraption which then transmitted words and music all the way from London. Mind you, you also needed to have a tall wireless pole, which had to be erected at the bottom of the garden, and the higher and further away from the house the pole was, the better the reception, A wire was then attached to the top of the pole, and brought into the house where it was connected to the wireless set. You had to have an earth wire as well, and this, after being attached to the set, was then taken out of the house via the window, in our case, and then the earth wire was plunged into the soil in the garden.

To be able to listen to this wonderful invention you also needed a pair of headphones or ear-phones, so really only one person at a time, could listen. Sometimes our step-father would call us, "Come quick, and hear this, it's wonderful." He would swivel the headphones round so that we each had one earpiece pressed against our young pink ears, we would sit there absolutely transfixed listening to this magic contraption, which brought, in some mysterious way, music and words from a distance of sixty miles or more.

One particularly windy day our step-father met old Fred Bones pushing his bike. "What's up then Fred?" our step-father called to him.

"That old wind's too strong fer I to ride me bike," he said, "but I'll bet you can hear London well today on that wireless thing of yourn, with this yer east wind a-blowin', thur yent nothin' to stop it."

Fred had been into our house and listened to our wireless set and had talked of nothing else since, but he was a bit too old in the head to ever understand how it worked.

Almost every week another family in the village would acquire a wireless set. "Ah missus," Bertha Botherum said to our Mother one day. "Guess who got one now? Them Arnolds, I see 'um puttin' the pole up, and Mrs Simmonds next door was looking that envious, I'll be they be the next to have one."

Bertha was the village gossip, there was nothing that escaped her eagle eye or ears. If you wanted to know what was going on, all you had to do was to ask Bertha. She was always sweeping the path in the front of her cottage, waiting for someone to come along to chatter to. She told her mother that is what she did it for.

"Ah, Mrs B," she said one day, "you don't know what loneliness is, when I gets fed up with me own company I just gets me broom and goes out to me front and starts sweeping, and before long somebody comes along for I to have a word with." Poor Bertha, she was her own worst enemy: some village folk would go the long way home just so that they would miss passing her cottage.

But apart from the pleasure that our wireless set brought us we still relied very much on the annual village activities for much of our enjoyment, and the highlight of the year was the parish tea always held on the Tuesday nearest Twelfth Night, a night when we tirelessly galloped round the parish room, joining in with the Lancers and Roger-de-Coverly. But to me the highlight of the evening was when Mr Franlin the M.C. announced, "And the next dance will be a Paul Jones," when I, as a fat fourteen year old, had the chance to dance with grown-up men, real good dancers some of them were too. Somehow I nearly always got fat Mr Spink; mind you, he waltzed beautifully and I seemed to ride round the room on his fat stomach, my feet just skimming the ground. We took up a lot of room, Mr Spinks and I, for as he twirled me round and round, his left arm, which lightly held my right was held outstreched, his eyes closed dreamily as we glided round and round to the strains of the Blue Danube. "Make a good dancer one day I shouldn't wonder," he puffed at me as the dance ended.

It was after one such parish tea that fate brought widower George Stokes and spinster Mary Ellen Brown together. Both of them lived in one of the nearby villages, but they did no more than pass the time of day with each other. George was a black-smith by trade, though now retired; his wife had been dead for about ten years. Mary Ellen had never married. Most of her life had been taken up by looking after her ailing mother and father. But after they died she surprised everyone by opening up a little shop in the front room of her house, where she sold the most delicious assortment of home-made sweets which she made in her kitchen. The small window in the front of the house was filled with dishes and bottles of Mary Ellen's sweets, and the wonderful smell that floated across the green when she was 'boiling up', tickled the nostrils of everyone who happened by.

She also made a goodly supply of rhubarb wine every year and some folks reckoned that she had got some stored away that was ten years old. Rhubarb was all that grew in her overgrown garden, which, folk said, looked like a forest of elephants' ears. The wine, Mary Ellen said, was "for medical purposes only". Occasionally she would give a bottle of it away, and those who had the privilege of sampling it said that it was some very potent stuff.

On this particularly cold frosty January night, George Stokes had stopped to chatter with some of his cronies after the parish tea festivities before cycling home, and when he did reach the village he noticed the light was still on in Mary Ellen's home. Coo, he thought, what wouldn't I give for a drop of Mary Ellen's celebrated rhubarb wine to warm me up! While these thoughts were running through his head, the light in the cottage went out and the village street seemed darker and colder than ever.

Whether it was the excitement of the evening, or the fact that Sam Finch had sent George on his way with a glass of his special parsnip wine, but we shall probably never know what made George act the way he did. He had heard that the famous rhubarb wine was kept locked up in the shed, next to the cottage. So he propped his bicycle up against Mary Ellen's gate and crept quietly into the yard. After a good deal of pulling and pushing, shoving and grunting, he managed to remove a couple of the wooden panels from the side of the shed. He squeezed himself through the opening and his eyes popped out like chapel hat pegs. There, neatly laid on their sides, were dozens and dozens of bottles, filled with the pale pink nectar. He struck a match, all the bottles were labelled and dated. He went along the neat rows striking match after match, reading as he went—1921, 1920, 1919. "Ah," he exclaimed. "This is the one, made May 1918, bottled July 1918, I'll try this one for a start," George muttered to himself. He pulled the cork, took a sniff, and then a long, long drink. This, thought George Stokes, is the wine of the gods, wine of a long-forgotten summer, heady and sweet.

By mid-morning the next day it was all round the village that George Stokes had spent the night with Mary Ellen Brown. At five o'clock that morning postman Tempest had seen George's bicycle propped up outside Mary Ellen's cottage and it was still there at midday when the baker went by.

"I don't believe it," the postman's wife said when her husband told her the news. "Mary Ellen wouldn't do such a thing."

"Well, why don't you go down to her shop and buy yerself two penneth of clove sweets," her husband retorted. "You will see for yerself then."

"You'd a thought he'd a had the decency to have took his bicycle round the back, out of the way, wouldn't you?" Bertha

Botherum said. "Downright disgraceful I calls it," she went on, "and at 'er age too, 'er's sixty if 'er's a day."

Poor Mary Ellen knew nothing about these tales that were flashing round the village like wildfire. Mind you, she had had two or three customers in for sweets that morning who had seemed highly amused about something. There was Mrs Crook, usually so friendly and chattery, but on this morning she had a job to even pass the time of day with Mary Ellen. Mrs Crook always came in on a Wednesday morning to buy her weekly half pound of humbugs which she took to her old mother who lived at Aston, and she fair flounced out of the shop with a very curt "good-morning". Then there was Jimmy Drake, he had actually winked at Mary Ellen as he went out.

About three o'clock that afternoon she went to the shed to get a few dry logs for the fire, and she noticed that some of the wooden panels had been forced from the side of it. "Now I wonder who did that," she thought. "Best to unlock the door first to see if anything has been stolen, then I must see if I can fix the wood back where it belongs."

Mary Ellen unlocked the door and pushed it open, then she let out a terrific scream, there, sprawled on the floor, surrounded by empty wine bottles, his mouth wide open, was George Stokes, and he looked as if he was dead.

Postman Tempest who was just going past on his afternoon rounds, heard the screaming, he threw his bicycle on to the grass verge and went running up the path to see what on earth was happening. He found Mary Ellen bending over the prostrate form of George Stokes, she was almost hysterical, crying over and over again, "He's dead, he's dead."

The postman bent down and touched the body, and sniffed, "He's dead all right Miss, dead drunk that's all. Come on," he said. "We had best get him into the house." Mary Ellen opened her mouth to protest but no words came out.

"Ah, thas wur 'e spent the night then," the postman said as they half carried, half dragged George into the cottage.

"We had best take him into the front parlour," Mary Ellen cried. "It's more comfortable in there." They managed to get him onto the horse-hair sofa where he stayed, in a kind of stupor for the best part of two days.

When she heard what the village had been saying about her and Mr Stokes, as she insisted on calling him, Mary Ellen blushed, in fact she went on blushing every time a villager dropped in to see how the patient was getting on. And although George was very ashamed of what he had done, he quite enjoyed the care and attention that Mary Ellen gave him during the next few days. Then it was back to his blacksmith's cottage, where, he admitted, he felt quite lonely.

On the following Sunday afternoon he knocked at Mary Ellen's door. "I've come to thank you again," he blurted out. "And to say how very sorry I am to have caused you so much trouble."

"You had better step inside out of the cold wind," she said. "I'm just going to make a cup of tea, you are welcome to join me, and I should push your bicycle round the back this time," she added, blushing shyly. "We don't want to start the villagers on again."

"I've brought you a bit of greenstuff from me garden," George said. "I've got that much I can't keep upsides with it." He handed her the bag of brussel sprouts and cabbages, and said, "I noticed that you hadn't got any in your garden."

When they spoke about it afterwards, neither of them could recall which of them it was who had suggested that George should give up his blacksmith's cottage and come and settle with Mary Ellen.

Within a few weeks George had sold his cottage and blacksmith's shop to Ern Brooks, a young man to whom he had taught the trade. It would do young Ern a treat, he and his wife were very keen to start up on their own.

Mary Ellen and George were married a few weeks later on St Valentine's Day, and they enjoyed several years of happy married bliss. Mary Ellen still made and sold her home-made sweets in

C

the front room, while George spent most of his time cultivating the garden. But he left no room for rhubarb, for although the wine drinking episode had brought them together, he vowed he would never touch another drop of the stuff as long as he lived, and strangely enough Mary Ellen did not seem to need any for medicinal purposes either.

"But what happened to all the wine that Mary Ellen had already made?" we asked our Mother who knew much more about the affair than we children.

"Well, come the following summer there was a special fête in the village to raise money for the church funds, so Mary Ellen and George offered the bottles of wine to be used in a raffle. My blessed, didn't they raffle tickets sell well, when folks knew that they stood a chance of winning a bottle of that wine. You see," our Mother went on, "that wine was a sort of symbol of revitalizing, giving the men back their youth and all that, at least thas what some people thought, and 'twas that wine as was blamed for a lot of things that followed in the villages around during the next year. Forty-year-old Mrs Snaith had twins, fifteen years after her last was born, Harry Patson went off with a housemaid from Lord B's estate, leaving his wife and seven children to fend for thurselves, and thur was ten weddings in as many months. And they reckons that all these parties had won bottles of Mary Ellen's wine.

"Of course," our Mother went on, "it was just a coincidence really, at least that's what I told Mary Ellen, cos her got quite perturbed about it. Folks be quick to make excuses for thur wrong-doings, that's what I always says. Mind you, I had a very small glass of it one day, down at Mrs Adnuts, and I have never tasted anything quite like it, it sort of lifted you up as it were. I got on my bicycle and I kind of floated home in a dream, but I soon came down to earth with a bump, for young Bunt had been digging up some potatoes and he had put the garden fork straight through his boot and into his big toe, so it was out with the carbolic soap and a good bowl of hot water. His toe came up like a balloon and he couldn't get his boot back on for a week, but it cleared up all right in the end. Mind you that boot of his let the wet in after that, and he hadn't had 'um long either. And do you know," she went on, "for years folks plagued the life out of Mary Ellen for the recipe for her rhubarb wine but she would never divulge how she made it, just as well, I suppose, if it was as potent as folks said it was."

# 4

# Hatching and Dispatching

One person who I was particularly fond of was Auntie Liza.

I can never remember anyone else living at 60 The Causeway except her; I suppose at some time or other there had been a Mr Green, but I do not remember him; no doubt the faded photograph on the chiffonier of the man with the droopy moustache was the man in Auntie Liza's life, though I never did hear her mention him.

Auntie Liza was not related to us, but just a very good friend of our Mother. She was the local midwife and had brought us all into the world; the youngest of our family, Denis, was the one to be most thankful to her. On a freezing cold night, with the roads covered with ice-packed snow, she half walked, half crawled, down to our cottage, to find that our Mother had already given birth to Denis, but she was too ill to try and break the umbilical cord which had almost strangled him. He was blue and purple when Auntie Liza, with her coat still on, rushed over and did whatever was necessary, but it was touch and go with young Denis for a while.

She was certainly a very handy person to have in the district, and the doctors had great respect for her. She used to say that she was in the "hatching and despatching" department of life, for as well as attending almost every birth in the area, she also laid folks out after they had died. But that was not all she did. People would come running to her when both children and grown-ups were ill. The latter services were all given freely, as most of her 'customers' were very poor, and even some of the mothers she attended had not any money to pay her for her services. "But," she used to say to our Mother, "it don't matter about a few shillings, as long as I've helped somebody, cos that's what we be here for right enough."

To me she always seemed rather old-fashioned, long-skirted, small-waisted and with a fat round chest; she reminded me of a rather large cottage loaf. Her grey hair was scraped back into a tight, tidy bun, and she had big soft brown eyes, and, to use our Mother's expression, "A heart as big as a bucket".

Auntie Liza's living-room was very small and she had quite a big table in the centre; this along with the rest of the furniture made it difficult for her to get round the room, so that she had to squeeze herself between things, shuffling sideways as she went.

"That boy wants holding over a tar barrel," she cried one day when she heard Ben, the youngest but one, coughing a croupy sort of cough.

"But they haven't started tarmac-ing the roads anywhere round here yet," our Mother replied. "As soon as I knows that they've started I shall be off, don't you worry. None of our others ever had the croup as bad as he, he's on night and day, we don't get hardly a minute's peace with him." It was widely believed that if a child could inhale the fumes that came from a boiling hot tar barrel it would help to break the phlegm and, of course, ease the cough or croup. And it was quite a common sight to see a red-faced coughing child, held by its equally red-faced mother, over a tar barrel when the workmen were re-surfacing the road.

I remember being suspended over one of those fearsome-look-ing things when I was about seven, kicking and screaming with fright in case I fell into that black boiling mass, but I proved too much for our Mother, strong as she was, and was handed over to a huge, red-faced roadman. "Come on, young Mollie," he said as he lifted me up: his arms were as strong and brown as tree-trunks. "Come and spit it up, it might be a tanner," he went on good-humouredly, as I coughed and spluttered. But I went on crying, longer and louder, when I found that, try as I may, I could not produce a sixpence. "Yer be," he said, grinning, handing me tup-pence, " 'Tis all I got till pay day."

One day Auntie Liza said to our Mother, "I reckon 'tis going to rain, my corn's playing me up summut dreadful, do you think you could remember to ask shepherd Spindlow fer a bit of sheep's wool, that do soothe my old corns, and soften um too, and then they'll drop awf after a while, 'tis the oil in the wool what does it you know." She knew lots of old-fashioned cures for many ordinary ailments.

"I got hold of this nice coat the other day, Kitty," she prattled on as they sipped their tea. "I thought that it might fit you a treat, you deserves one Lord knows." She brought out the soft, brown coat. Our Mother looked at it lovingly, "Ah, much as I'd love it, I'd better have it altered for Bet, she's growing that fast the one she's wearing fits her so tight you'd think she'd been poured into it. Mollie can have hers and I'll get Sally Castle to alter this one for Bet, that 'ull do her nicely for a couple of years then."

The better-off people that Auntie Liza attended often gave her their cast-offs, and although she did not need much for herself she never refused, knowing that we would be glad of almost any-thing.

"And this," she went on, "might make them two youngest a pair of trousers each." She held up a long navy blue serge skirt.

"Aah, that it will," Mother cried joyfully. "I got a very easy pattern that Auntie Maggie let me have, I'll cut them out tonight when they've all gone to bed, that won't take me long to run um up."

"Don't ferget to line um," Auntie Liza said. "Else you'll have um with sore bums first time they wears um."

Round the fire-guard was an assortment of beautifully laundered baby clothes. Hard-up mothers knew that if they could not afford all the needs of their new-born babies, Liza Green would see that the newcomer was properly clothed, at least during the period that she was attending the mother and child. This was done out of the kindness of her own heart. Over the years she had collected day-gowns, night-gowns, back-flannels and minute vests. As soon as the clothes were finished with, Auntie Liza had them back, laundered them and stowed them away in the rush basket ready for the next time.

Our Mother looked at the tiny garments, "Still finding plenty of customers then, Liza?" she asked.

"Ah, poor devils, some of um are too," she replied, "not a penny in the house to buy a bit of bread and three or four hungry mites already to feed, there's more poverty in this town than anybody realizes," she went on. "I does what I can for um, but half the mothers ent had a decent meal for weeks, so how can you expect the babies to be strong and healthy. I was along at Mrs Smith's yesterday," she went on, "just had her ninth she have."

"You means Mrs Quaker Oats Smith?" our Mother asked.

"Ah, that's the one," Auntie Liza said smilingly.

We all knew the story about the Quaker Oats, but at that tender age I wondered what they found to laugh at. Apparently during the war this Mrs Smith went to the Doctor; she explained to him that she was feeling bad and getting quite fat. The Doctor examined her and said, "You know what's wrong with you, don't you? You're going to have a baby, quite soon by the look of things."

"But I can't," she cried. "My husband's bin in France for a twelve-month or more and I've never been out with another man. Could you be mistaken, doctor?" she asked, "perhaps it's summat as I've ett as makes I feel so bad."

"What have you been eating?" the doctor asked, humouring her.

"Well, I have been eating a lot of Quaker Oats," the weeping woman told him.

"Well then," the doctor replied, "it must have been the little man on the packet, cos you're having a baby all right."

Just then there was a hammering on the door and a neighbour poked her head inside, "Oh, Auntie Liza Green, could you come quick, our Freddy's caught his fingers in my mangle, and I don't know what to do, he's crying summut terrible."

"Shan't be long, Kitty," she called to our Mother as she went out the door. "Just pour yourself another cup of tea," and she went rushing down the path with the tearful woman.

In about ten minutes Auntie Liza was back. "The boy's fingers ent badly hurt," she said, "there's nothing broken, no skin cracked or anything, I think the poor little chap was more frightened than anything. I got his mother to hold his hand down in a bowl of cold water, that u'll ease it and fetch the swelling down. I told his mother to make a nice cup of tea, it would do her and the boy good, but she hadn't a bit of tea in the house. Here," she said to me, "just pop along to the cottage, fifth one from here, with this screw of tea," and she came to the door to make sure that I took it to the right place.

"I promised you some drunken husbands* next time you called," Auntie Liza said, "I'll just pop out and get some while I thinks of it." She returned in a few minutes with some green plants. "Here you are, Kitty, just push 'um in the wall anywhere and they'll grow a treat, and flower next year if you leaves 'um be, course you knows the old saying, don't you, that these plants u'll only survive in a home where the woman wears the trousers," she said laughingly.

"Oh, I must just tell you about old Jim Paine," Auntie Liza prattled on. "At last I've persuaded him to get some false teeth, 'e bin suffering summut dreadful with indigestion fer years, I told him 'twas because he couldn't chew his food properly. Well, he's fitted up with some now, but they be taking a bit of getting used to by all accounts. He was in the garden planting his "sharlots" as he calls shallots, when I went by on me bike, so I jumps awf and goes back and asked him how he was getting on with his "artificials" and he said the funniest thing, he said, 'Well they be no good fer 'etting' but champion fer 'oldin' me pipe.' "

It was nice to listen to Auntie Liza and our Mother chattering

* Drunken husbands—house leeks.

and laughing over a cup of tea; we visited her quite often, for she only lived in the town a couple of miles away. Whenever we called she always found us children a biscuit apiece, always the same sort, digestive, which she kept in a pretty china biscuit barrel that stood on the chiffonier next to the photo of the man with the droopy moustache. The biscuit barrel was white with delicate pink and blue flowers on and pale green leaves.

"Ah, old Mrs Wafler gave me that," Auntie Liza told our Mother when she remarked on its beauty. "That's a band of silver round the edge," she went on. "You shall have that, Kitty, when anything happens to me, cos I knows you'd appreciate it." But when the time came our Mother did not mention it to the tighted-lipped niece who quickly cleared out the crowded cottage after Auntie Liza had been laid to rest in the nearby cemetery.

"After all, they'd have thought I was cadging," our Mother said. "But never mind," she went on, "I got some lovely memories of her, I shall miss her and so will a lot of folk. Ah, if anybody have earned their harp and crown, she have," she said tearfully.

Quite often before we went into the town, our Mother would pick a bunch of flowers from our garden and take them and lay them on the otherwise deserted grave. We all missed Auntie Liza very much, and it did not seem right to pass the cottage, where the window had always been packed tight with ferns and the little room stuffed with furniture, and not go in.

Each Christmas time, when we were all living at home, our Mother used to receive a Christmas card simply signed "Flora". She would open the card, and read the signature, smile sadly and say, "poor dear", then promptly throw the card on the fire. She never said who the mysterious Flora was, and we knew, the way she looked when she read it, that we were not supposed to probe either. And so the years went by, Christmases came and went and the cards kept coming. Then one Christmas she did not get one. I asked her why. "I knew I shouldn't receive one this year, neither shall I ever get one again," she replied sadly. "But then, maybe it's all for the best."

Whatever "the best" was I did not learn until many years afterwards. I do not think any other member of our family ever knew, maybe because none of them were ever as inquisitive as me.

One year I was helping our Mother to get her Christmas cards away, for in her later years with her memory failing, she was never quite sure who she had sent to. I happened to mention the card that she used to have each Christmas time signed Flora, and the fact that she had never told us about it.

She thought for a moment and then said, "Well, I can tell you about it now, because there is nobody alive today that was involved," She went on, "I hated having secrets from the family, but a promise is a promise and I've kept that for nearly fifty years."

"It all happened before you was born, before we came to live in Ducklington," she said. "We had rather a nice house in Witney I'd only got young Bern and Bunt at the time. There was only thirteen months between them, so they were babies together as you might say. I used to push them for miles; every day I used to take them out for a long walk. Well, on this particular day that I'm telling you about, I had planned to walk four miles to visit a tiny church away in the fields. By the time I reached the village both the boys were fast asleep, so I pushed the pram in to the shade, making sure that Bern was safetly strapped in. Bunt of course was still at the lying down stage, so he was safe enough. Then I tiptoed into the church. Oh, it was so small and beautiful. Then I heard the sound of giggling and scuffing coming from the vestry and I thought, 'If that was my children messing about in church they would get a good hiding.' So I went up to the door, which was ajar, about to tell the children off for larking about in God's house. But it wasn't children larking about, it was the churchwarden, a married man with two children, and the vicar's daughter, in the act of love making.

"I turned on my heel and walked quickly out of the church and stood for a moment in the warm sunshine absolutely numbed with shock. Then I caught hold of the pram and was just about to rush out of the churchyard gate, when a young and very beautiful girl came out.

" 'Oh please, please don't go. Please stop and talk to me for a moment,' she called to me.

" 'If you want to do that sort of thing' I said to her, 'I would have thought you would have had the decency to have chosen somewhere different, that's all. Anyway where's *he* gone?" I asked her. I knew the man by sight and had heard of his amorous goings on. "Gone sculking off home I suppose, leaving you to face the music,' I cried.

"Then the girl broke out sobbing, 'Please sit down, I must talk to someone.' So we made our way to the old wooden seat set against the church.

"I put my arm round the young girl's shoulders which shook with sobs as she told me her story. She had just finished three years at college and after the summer vacation she was going to Scotland where she had taken the post to tutor three sons of a wealthy family who lived in the Highlands. Her mother had died two years ago, she was an only child, and it would break her father's heart if he found out about her and Mr Brookson. The affair, she said, had gone on all the summer. She met him every day, always in the church where the love making took place.

" 'But,' I said to her, 'you must have been out of your mind to have started such a thing, and why don't you put a stop to it now?'

"Then the girl went on to say that Mr Brookson had threatened to tell her father that it was her who was pestering him if she didn't turn up every day.

"So I said to her, 'What happens if he puts you in the family way?'

" 'Well,' she said, 'I think he already has, it's only a matter of two weeks, but I've never been late before. What am I going to do? I dare not tell my father or Mr Brookson.'

"Well, I talked to the girl for ages, imploring her to tell her father, but she said that she would rather kill herself than bring shame to him in the village where he was so respected. In the end she decided, and I agreed with her, that she should go to Scotland and take the job, at least until Christmas. Then leave saying that she had another post to go to. She could find some quiet place to stay until the baby was born, and then arrange to have it adopted and no one, at least in this part of the country, would ever know any different.

"Then the girl said, 'But what about the Christmas holiday, my father would expect me home for that.'

"Well, I told her, she could probably just about make it without suspicion if she bundled herself up in woollies and furs, but she would have to tell him she was changing jobs. You see, he might have begun to get worried if the postmark on her letters to him was different.

"Fortunately the girl had plenty of money. Her mother had left her some, so too had an aunt, on her mother's side.

"Well, the hot day wore on, the boys woke up hungry. I was breast feeding Bunt and this simply horrified the girl. 'Don't worry,' I told her 'there will be no need for you to do this, there's plenty of patent baby food on the market for those who have the money to pay for it.'

"We talked for hours in that quiet churchyard about the girl's future. Of course she wanted to write to me regular like. But I said to her, 'Oh no, you mustn't do that.' No, that would have never done. You see, I would have had to explain her letters to your father and the rest of the family. So I suggested that she should just send me a card every Christmas and I should know that she was all right.

"Mind you, she was a bit worried about Mr Brookson, you know, that he might talk.

" 'My dear child,' I said to her 'you must forget you ever met the man, if that's possible. Don't you think that you are the first young girl that he's led astray because you are not. He's got a terrible reputation, and him pretending to be a good churchman too.' Evidently the stories of his conquests had not reached her father's ears but everybody else knew. It was his wife and children that I felt so sorry for, and the girl of course.

"The warm sunny afternoon wore on, the clock on the church tower struck three and I said that I would have to make tracks for home. I'd got a meal to cook and have on the table ready for when your father got home. I left the tearful, beautiful, young girl in the churchyard, after making her promise that she would do nothing foolish, and that every year she would send a card at Christmas time to assure me that all was well."

"But what did happen to her?" I asked.

"Well, she had a child, a little girl, but it only lived for two days, which was just as well I suppose. She might not have wanted to have parted with it and then the truth would have had to come out.

"But Flora never married," she went on, "She continued her governessing, and taught the children of several wealthy families. She came home about twice a year to see her father. I met her in Witney once when I was doing a bit of shopping, we chatted for a while but she seemed so sad and lonely. I wondered if I had advised her rightly. Perhaps it would have been best if she had made a clean breast of it, but then there was her father to think of and Mr Brookson's wife and children. The poor girl died some years ago, in a London hospital I think. I suppose she must have been about fifty. Anyway they brought her back to the village. I cycled over to the funeral and the first person I met was that old devil Mr Brookson, and he looked proper foolish when he saw me. He siddled up to me and spoke all smarmsy like. 'Hello, Mrs Butler,' he said, 'a sad day for us all isn't it?' I never answered him, but I just gave him one of my withering looks and he did not know where to put his face. He soon cleared off after that and I never saw him again.

"But mind you," our Mother went on, "I heard about his unfortunate family from time to time. He had three children, two girls and a boy, and they all turned out bad, they probably inherited their father's lustful ways. One of his girls had two love children and nobody ever knew who was the father of them. The second girl had a love child too, then she went off and lived with a married man who had put her in the family way. The lad was no better. Twice he was taken to court by young girls who he had got into trouble, then he ended up living with an amorous married woman, years older than himself, and died at forty-eight, a worn-out, lustful man. Ah you know what the good Book says," our Mother continued. "The sins of the fathers upon the children, and I reckon that's what that was all right."

# 5

# China Dogs and China Cups

Our Auntie Rosie and Uncle Charlie lived in a village about four miles from Ducklington. They always reminded me of a couple of porker pigs because they were both pink and fat with a clean, scrubbed look.

Their snug, warm low-thatched home called "Walnut Tree Cottage" was like a fairyland to us children. It was filled with china dogs, brasses and copper and brightly coloured antimacassars, and tinkling vases with glass icicles dangling all round them. And the fire grate always shone black and gleaming. Our Mother used to say, "You could see to comb your hair in Auntie Rosie's grate." She had a set of shiny brass fire-irons too (we only had steel ones) and when that big old fire was lit, the flames seemed to wink and blink in every piece of brass and copper, glass and china.

Both Auntie Rosie and Uncle Charlie had worked very hard all their lives, but now, in their late sixties they just jogged along happily from one day to the next, and seemed to grow more pink and rounded as the years rolled by.

They were only very slightly related to us on our father's side, and they had always been most kind to us all.

Every year about October time Uncle Charlie would arrive at our house on his creaky, old, upright bicycle. "We be killing a pig on Saturday, Kitty," he would say to our Mother. "You will be a-coming over as usual, won't you?"

We knew that we should come back from their house simply loaded with the pig's chitterlings, its head and trotters and some spare-rib. We always invited them to our pig killing, but they would never take much of ours. "No, Kitty," Auntie Rosie would say, when our Mother tried to press her into taking some of the fresh meat, "You got more mouths to feed than we have, I'll just take a little bit of the pig's fry for our tea tonight, that will do we just fine."

We in Ducklington had Mr Humphries who came and killed our pigs, but Auntie Rosie and Uncle Charlie used to have an old fellow called Tom Arthurs to kill theirs. Old Tom repeated everything twice. We thought that he did it "a purpuss", as Auntie Rosie called it, but Uncle Charlie said that it was just a silly habit that he had got into. Habit or not we used to laugh at him, not unkindly, but just because he was such a cheerful old chap who seemed to delight in making us chuckle.

Uncle Charlie and old Tom were usually just trying to lift the squealing pig onto the wooden bench when we arrived on the scene. They had erected it down at the far end of the garden next to the pigsty, we could hear old Tom's voice above the frightened squeals of the animal shouting, "Tick t'un Charlie, tick t'un, Charlie." (stick to him, Charlie.)

"Damn good pig s'now, damn good pig s'now" (damn good pig you know). "Ten or twelve score I'll bet, ten or twelve score I'll bet." The pig was on the bench at last but still struggling, "Burr on 'is ass a bit, burr on 'is ass a bit" (put a bit more weight on his backside so that the kicking would be useless), old Tom bellowed Now ready for the killing, he shouted again, "Hand I that old knife, hand I that old knife," then old Tom 'stuck' the pig. "Thas got the old bugger, thas got the old bugger" he shouted triumphantly as the poor lifeless animal lay there.

We jumped about and squealed and laughed all the time old Tom was shouting instructions to Uncle Charlie. "Dump 'im on 't straw Charlie, dump 'im on 't straw, burn 'is bloody bristles awf, burn 'is bloody bristles awf," he cried, setting fire to the bolton of straw where the animal lay. The men straightened their aching backs for a few minutes and the air was filled with the smell of burning

Ducklington church and school with the village pond in the foreground

The village today, hardly changed since the author was a girl

The author's father and father of Bern, Bunt and Betty. He is standing beside the local doctor's car of which he was a chauffeur

as smoke wafted across the garden stinging our eyes. Then they lifted the body on to the rough bench so that old Tom could start to cut it up.

We were still giggling an hour later, when Auntie called us into dinner. We had salt belly pork, from their last year's pig. Auntie had baked it in a huge tin in the old fire oven, it was covered with sliced onions and sliced potatoes and simply oozed with fat. Then there was a jam rolly polly for afters.

Old Tom had his dinner with us: he was still repeating himself even at the dinner table. "Damn good cook s'now, damn good cook s'now, fair blowed out I be, fair blowed out I be," he said patting his drum-like stomach.

"A nice cup of tea before we starts work again will just put us right I reckon," Auntie Rosie said, as she lifted the kettle on to the fire. "Let me see," she said to old Tom, "if I remembers rightly you likes your tea on the strong side, don't you?"

"Yes missus, I do that, yes missus, I do that," he replied, "I likes it so thick, you could trot a mouse across it, I likes it so thick you could trot a mouse across it." At this remark, we absolutely doubled up helpless with laughter, with childlike visions of harnessed mice trekking across seas of strong tea, with old Tom holding on to the reins.

Before we left for home Auntie Rosie loaded our old pram up with "pig's innards, yead and fit", as old Tom called the chitterlings, head and feet. There was just room in the pram for Denis, the youngest, to ride with Betty and I lending our Mother a hand in pushing it. We had left the rest of the family at home, for although Auntie Rosie and Uncle Charlie made us very welcome to their cottage, there was not room for us all at the same time, so we took it in turns to visit them.

The next day or two after our visit to them was very busy for our Mother as she made the brawn from the pig's head and feet and cleaned and cooked the chitterlings. She also made some lovely pig's head broth, from the liquor left over after the head had been cooked. Into this she would put plenty of carrots, onions and tur-

nips and a good bunch of mixed herbs and a couple of meat cubes
to give it a bit of colour. "Look at them lovely pheasants' eyes
on top of it," she would say before she dished it up. She called the
glistening minute rings of fat that floated on the top of the broth
pheasants' eyes. "Of course," our Mother told us one day, "if you
was cooking soup or stew for the gentry, you would have to get
rid of every scrattock (scrap) of fat, but we 'ent gentry and it's
them pheasants' eyes that keeps us going."

During all the visits that we made to Auntie Rosie's and Uncle
Charlie's home, it never seemed to alter, the warm comfortable
living-room always appeared exactly the same to me. On the big,
high mantle-shelf over the fireplace there was a wonderful assortment of things. In the centre was a chiming clock, given to Auntie
as a wedding present, by The Honourable Elizabeth Hammetly, a
lady for whom she worked as a nannie for several years. The clock
played hymns at twelve o'clock, and again at three, six and nine
o'clock. Two tunes it played: "Rock of Ages", and "Fight the
Good Fight". I can still seem to hear Auntie's high-pitched voice
singing to the accompaniment of those tunes.

One day when she was singing "Fight the Good Fight" I burst
out crying. "What's the matter, my little love?" she cried, running to my side.

"I don't want you to go off fighting, Auntie," I sobbed. "I wants
you to stay here." You see, the only fighting I had heard about was
from snatches of conversation when our step-father talked about
the war and "trenches full of dead men all piled on top of one
another", and I certainly did not want Auntie Rosie to join
them.

On the shelf next to the clock was a fat dumpy casket like a tea-
caddie, tin it was, and painted on two sides, in colour were the
words Mazawattee Tea, but on the other two opposite sides was
the picture of an old lady dressed in a long skirt, she had a shawl
over her shoulders and a mob cap on her head and, sitting on her
lap was a little girl, dressed just like the grannie, and the child
had the old lady's reading glasses perched on her nose and they

were both drinking a large cup of tea. I expect there was a caption written underneath; if there was I have forgotten it.

There were also two tallish vases, black with pink roses on them, these were Uncle's spill jars. These spills were made by folding up thin strips of newspaper. Then, when he wanted to light his pipe or Auntie wanted to light the lamp or candles, they just took a spill from the jar and lit it from the fire, and then lit your pipe, lamp or candle with it. And in this way a box of matches would last for ages, because the only time you struck one was to light the fire each day. Every cottager reckoned to have a goodly supply of home-made spills on their mantleshelf in those days.

Then at each end of the shelf there was a beautiful china dog, white with reddish patches on them. The reddish patches, Auntie told me, were what made them valuable, because it was a special colour that the makers of the dogs had created.

Some years later when both Auntie Rosie and Uncle Charlie were ailing she told me that when she and Uncle were "dead and gone" the dogs were to go to our Mother. "But Auntie," I said, "you and Uncle are not going anywhere yet." I could not seem to use the words "dead" or "dying"—they seemed so final.

Yet, in their case the end came quite quickly, quicker than anyone had imagined. One evening they were sitting by the fire chatting away quite happily, then Auntie Rosie asked Uncle a question and when he did not answer she looked up at him and he had gone, died peaceful like, just sitting there. Poor Auntie Rosie never got over the shock, and the very day he was to be buried she had a heart attack and died the next day.

Wisely Auntie had left a note to say that her dear friend Kitty was to have the two china dogs. Unfortunately our Mother was unable to go to the funeral. She had to take young Ben to the Radcliffe Hospital to have his adenoids and tonsils out on that very day.

So our step-father said that he would ride over and attend Auntie Rosie's funeral and pick up the china dogs afterwards.

He carefully wrapped the dogs up in plenty of newspaper, put them into a bag and strapped them on the carrier of his bicycle and started for Ducklington.

He was about half-way home and coming through a hamlet, when suddenly there was a commotion in the street, the few people about scattered quickly as a runaway horse pulling a cart came careering down the road, the young lad holding the reins was shouting for help at the top of his voice. Quick as a flash our step-father stood his bicycle up against the wall and took a flying leap at the frightened horse as it passed him, grabbing it by the neck where he hung on tightly until he brought the animal to a standstill.

The driver was only a lad of fourteen and of course not very experienced with horses, especially such a frisky one as this. Our step-father told the lad that he would drive the animal back to the farm for him if he wished, and he had a few hard words to say to the farmer too for sending a youngster out with such a fresh horse. When our step-father got back to where he had left his bicycle it had disappeared, china dogs and all. He made enquiries at the cottages near but no one had seen anything. He reported it to the police but we never heard another word about it.

We all thought our Mother would fly into a terrible temper about the loss of the bike and the lovely dogs, but she did not, in fact she was very proud of him for saving the boy's life. Later that evening I crept upstairs to find her crying quietly to herself. I made to comfort her but she brushed me aside. "Go on," she said, "I can't do with anybody's sympathy just now, I shall be all right in the morning," and come next day she was her old cheerful self again, but it was ages before anyone even mentioned the dogs.

As to the bicycle, our step-father had to have one to get backwards and forwards to work, and within twenty-four hours he had got all the bits and pieces together and had built himself another one. He found an old bike frame in a ditch that someone had thrown away, some handlebars which he had saved from a previous old bike, and a neighbour gave him an old saddle. Wheels he just could not afford to buy, so Bern and he went off to an old refuse pit and searched over the rubbish until they found some; mind you, some of the spokes were missing so he went off to Witney and bought a few new ones which only cost a few pence which he put in himself, but he just had to buy tubes, tyres and a chain. I think he had an idea who the thief was, but without proof he was not able to do anything about it.

Years later, long after our step-father had died and we had all left home, an elderly woman knocked at the door of our Mother's bungalow, thrust a parcel into her hands, and mumbled, "This is yourn," and made to rush away. Our Mother called her back and asked her indoors and over a cup of tea the poor frightened woman told her story.

It was her husband, she said, who had died tragically the year before, who had stolen the bicycle and the dogs. Apparently the man had been out of work for eighteen months, they had six children and were near to starving. He had at last got the chance of a job, seventeen miles away and he could earn nearly three pounds a week. The problem was, how was he to get there. He could have walked if he had been properly fed, but the poor man was half starved and would not have been able to hold the job down for long had he had to walk to work. Of course when he got the cycle home and found the china dogs on the back, they just did not know what to do, so they hid them away in a drawer and there they had stayed all these years. As she listened to the old lady's story our Mother took the china dogs out of the very newspaper in which our step-father had so carefully wrapped them. She stroked them fondly and then re-wrapped them up again. Handing them to the old lady our Mother said, "You take them my dear, take them and enjoy them, and thank you for having the heart to bring them back after all this time. It's a funny thing," she went on, "I don't bear you no ill will. Mind you," she said with a smile, "there's no knowing what I might have done a few years back, but we all gets a bit wiser as we gets older, don't we?"

Yes, our Mother had certainly mellowed over the years, and the reappearance of the china dogs reminded me of the time when I lost a cup at a summer school treat—a beautiful china cup it was too, it had a brilliant cock pheasant painted on it and a fancy handle. It had belonged to our Gramp, our Mother's father who had lived at Sherbourne. I think it was a 'fairing', brought back from Stow on the Wold fair, and it was nearly one hundred years old.

When we had a school treat at Ducklington, all the children were asked to bring their own mug or cup. And what an assortment of old cups and mugs turned up on those days. Many families, like ourselves, were very poor and only had a few cracked cups to their name, some handleless too. It was my last but one year at school I remember, I was thirteen at the time. Besides having to find a cup for me our Mother also had to find one for Mick, Ben and Denis. They went off with their cups, which were carefully labelled with their names written on a piece of tape which was tied on to the handles.

Our Mother looked at the poor assortment of cups left. "I can't let you go to the treat with any of them," she cried. "Look, I'll let you use Gramp's cup if you will promise to bring it back here in one piece." "Yes, yes," I cried excitedly, "I promise." I was so pleased to think that I was old enough to be entrusted with Grampy's special cup. It was *never* used for drinking, but kept as an ornament on the shelf. One highlight of the summer school treat was the country dancing on the rectory lawn, in some of them, all the children took part, but the special dances were performed by a select few.

This year I had not been chosen to dance along with the girls of my age, and I was feeling a bit put out about it, and had already threatened to fight one or two of them because of it. But I soon forgot about the dancing when the races began, being "one a they long legged Woodleys" as we were called, I romped home first in all the races, with the gentle girls who had taken part in the dances looking on enviously at my success.

The shadows had already begun to lengthen on the rectory lawn when we were told to gather up our belongings and make for home. I made a bee-line for the big cedar tree where I had carefully put my Gramp's precious cup—it was gone.

We looked everywhere for it, even the rector joined in the search, "Perhaps one of your brothers or Micky has taken it home," they suggested hopefully. But I knew as I crawled home that the cup was lost and I was already crying when I reached our cottage.

Some years after I had lost the cup, I heard that Mrs Compford was bad in bed, so I called to see if I could do an errand for her or maybe a bit of house work. She was very ill, with a bed downstairs in the small living-room. We chatted for a few minutes, then she asked me to get her a drink of water. I reached across to the crowded dresser for a glass, there in the centre was a lovely china cup, it had a brilliant cock pheasant painted on it and a fancy handle. For one split second I was back on the rectory lawn, the day was hot and sunny and I had just threatened to fight Sally Compford because she had been chosen to dance and I had not, the panic when I could not find the cup and the hiding that followed, and besides that I had to go to bed at six o'clock every night during the rest of that summer holiday, and the fact that for years I was never allowed to forget that I had lost the precious cup.

I got the drink for the old lady; her only daughter had married an American and she had gone overseas with him. She had been sent for, but no one knew whether or not she would be back in time to see her old mother alive again. It might *not* have been my Grampy's cup, but I would have bet every penny I had that it was.

# 6

## *Where the Windrush Flows*

"Smells are surer than sounds or sights
To make your heartstrings crack"

Those are the opening lines of one of Rudyard Kipling's poems, and the words are very true. Certain smells do bring back memories of incidents that happened years ago.

The smell of freshly made mint sauce, stewed rhubarb and pomanders always reminds me of a special trip that we made to our Auntie Mary's, who lived, as our step-father used to say, "within spitting distance of us". Mind you, there would have had to have been a good following wind, for spit to have ever reached her house from ours, because it was at least two miles away. And although we often popped over to see her and she would call and see us on her way back home, after she had been shopping in the town, it is this one special springtime visit that I remember best.

We had never had a meal at Auntie Mary's before. It was usually just a cup of tea and one of her home-made biscuits and sometimes in summer a glass of her special lemonade, made with real lemons.

But it was this super, sunny Sunday morning when we were all invited to dinner that stands out in my mind, for at no other time can I remember having Sunday dinner anywhere else but at home, except when I went to stay with our relations at Sherbourne.

We set out about eleven o'clock, Mother, step-father, Bern, Bunt, Betty and myself, with Mick our step-sister in the pram. This was before our step-brothers Ben and Denis were born.

The reason for this particular invitation was because Auntie

Mary had just received the sum of two hundred pounds which had been left to her by a generous employer. She had been in service for several years, and this money was from Lord and Lady Bacters. Auntie Mary had been a lady's maid to her Ladyship. Now both of them had died and all the servants who had been in their employment had received small bequests.

When she heard the news Auntie Mary said to our Mother, "Kitty I should like to share a bit of the money with you and the family, so I wants you all to come over to Sunday dinner and tea." She knew this would indeed be a super treat for us, for in those days seldom was a family of seven invited out all together, specially to Sunday dinner.

And it was that smell that welcomed us as we arrived at her house that I shall never forget. Auntie had just finished making the mint sauce; on the table was a wooden chopping board, white as snow from continuous scrubbings and dryings in the sun. There were still some leaves and stalks left on it and the room was filled with the smell of bruised mint and the sharp, contrasting smell of vinegar. And floating through from the kitchen came the unmistakable smell of stewed rhubarb, the first of the season, all pink and tender. She always put a slice of lemon in with her ruhbarb while it was cooking, which gave it a lovely flavour.

Pleased to see us, Auntie Mary fussed around us all. We children were each given a glass of her home-made lemonade. For our Mother there was a glass of parsley wine, and our step-father a bottle of beer that Auntie had bought specially.

"Just hark at that darned bird," Auntie Mary remarked as we sipped our refreshments, "he's been on since four o'clock this morning cooing about."

"Is it a dove or a pigeon?" she asked.

"A collared dove," our step-father said.

"Hark at it," she said again. The bird cooed on regardless, "Coo oo oo cowee." "My toe bleeds, Betty", we said it sang, but Auntie Mary said that it was "You can't do it, Suzie", while our step-father said that is was "not tonight, Lisa." Whatever it was there was no stopping the courting song of the lovesick bird high up in the old elm tree by the side of her house.

We watched Auntie Mary set the table. The cloth was white and stiff and shiny with starch. Never had we eaten at such a table. Every knife and fork matched as well as the spoons, and even the plates and dishes were all the same pattern, not like in our house. Our cutlery left much to be desired as did our crocks; often you had to get up and swill the plate that you had had your meat and vegetables on, so that you could use it for your pudding, we were that short.

Suddenly it was dinner time. Our step-father was asked to carve the leg of lamb. Slivers and slivers of pink, tender meat slipped off that sharp carving knife. It was a lovely meal with crispy baked potatoes and fluffy mashed ones, spring cabbage and that super, succulent lamb, covered with mint sauce. For pudding we had the choice of stewed rhubarb and custard or "Whitsuntide pie"—a green gooseberry pie.

The meal over and the washing up done we all sat down and had a cup of coffee, a thing unheard of in our house.

Auntie Mary had never married, but she was not the usual prim old maid, she was cheerful and happy and, as she said, she was an old maid from choice, she had had plenty of offers, but was very content as she was. Auntie Mary's mother had worked at Osborne House for a while during the reign of Queen Victoria, and that afternoon Auntie Mary showed us a treasure that was to become mine. When the old Queen died, some of her dresses were cut up, and pieces given to the staff as momentoes. This was a panel from a very lovely dress, black, covered with hundreds of minute beads embroidered on to look like bunches of pink roses. It must have been taken from one of Queen Victoria's earlier dresses, because it is reputed that she wore black for many of her later years.

The reason I was presented with this treasure was because Auntie Mary was my godmother. I suspect too that it was she who gave me the name of Victoria.

It was from Auntie Mary that I learned the art of making pomanders. She always gave our Mother one at Christmas time. I called on her one day when she was busily making some for her Christmas gifts. "Here," she said, "you can make the holes in the oranges with this bodkin and push the cloves into the hole, just leaving the thick end of the clove sticking out." This done we then rolled the clove-filled oranges in equal quantities of orris root and cinnamon. Then we carefully wrapped each orange separately in greaseproof paper and stacked them in Auntie's spare bedroom, where they stayed for six weeks. By then they were ready to have a bit of pretty ribbon tied on them before being given away.

Before we left Auntie Mary's on that special day she gave us all a small gift. Our Mother had a rather nice blue and silver brooch, our step-father a tie-pin, Bern and Bunt each had a horn-handled pocket knife, and we three girls a locket and chain apiece. Then it was back home to Ducklington while it was still light.

We met several families out for their Sunday night walk, and some courting couples too. Then we came upon Fred Since, leaning on his bicycle evidently waiting for a someone to come along. We stopped to chatter with him.

"Who is it tonight then, Fred," our step-father asked.

"Ah wouldn't you like to know, but I 'ent telling," he replied, laughing loudly.

Poor Fred, he was a bit on the simple side. Our Mother's description of him was "that he had got all his buttons on, but they had never been tightened up". She would only say this at home, never to his face or to other folk.

"I see you got your swank handkerchief showing, Fred," our Mother remarked. Fred loved it if you noticed things like that.

"Oh yes, missus," Fred replied in his slow, drawling voice. "I allus 'as two hankchers when I goes out dressed up like, thas one fer blowin' and one fer showin'."

"And what's this I hear about you going out regular with a young lady in the town, Fred?" she asked him kindly.

"Well," Fred replied, blushing to the roots of his hair. "Well, I

can't say as I goo's with 'er mind, I rides round the town a time
or two on me bike with 'er, but I can't say as I goo's with 'er, well
not to say goo's with 'er like."

If we kids met Fred down in the village we would tease the life
out of him. "Got yer collar and tie on tonight then, Fred?" we
had called knowing darn well what the answer would be. "I never
reckons to wear one all the week, but come Sunday I always puts
me collar and hames on." Fred worked with horses and would
never have thought of saying collar and *tie*.

Poor Fred did not have a chance really. Apparently both his
mother and father were a bit on the simple side too. And they
used to quarrel and fall out very often. One day when they had had
a particularly nasty row and Fred's father was a bit more fed up
than usual, he went into the local butchers and said, "I wish somebody 'ud shoot me or something and put me out of my misery."
So the butcher, jokingly, picked up his meat cleaver and made to
chop the man's head off. "Oh don't do it now," he said, "wait till
I be asleep, it won't hurt so much then."

And once, when Fred was a youngster, he was apparently very
ill and his mother called the doctor in. There was young Fred laid
in bed white as a sheet and motionless. The doctor took one look
at him and said, "I think he's dead."

"That I byent," Fred said.

But his mother answered, "Now then Fred, don't argue, Doctor
knows best."

With parents like that Fred could not help getting into all sorts
of scrapes, and the lads of the village used to set him up to do all
sorts of things, and Fred was simple enough to do them.

One night a gang of boys got hold of an old railway sleeper and
dared Fred to push it down old Mr Paine's chimney. They knew
that every night the old man, who was as deaf as a post, used to
stay up in the evening until every bit of fire had burnt out in his
grate. The lads helped Fred to get the sleeper on to the roof and
then he slowly let it down the chimney. One fellow was looking
through Mr Paine's window, so that he could let Fred know when

the end of the sleeper reached the flames. Of course, all railway sleepers are treated with creosote and once the fire got hold of it it went like a torch. The villagers helped to quell the fire by form-ing a human chain of buckets of water, with one man tipping it straight down the chimney, until the fire brigade arrived from the town. But nobody let on who had played the rotten trick on the old man. Even Fred, for once, was fly enough not to own up either.

Another time the lads got hold of an old lemonade bottle, the sort that had a glass marble in, which kept the contents airtight. They filled it with carbide, sealed it up and then got Fred to leave it outside Claggy Weston's cottage. Then they all hurried a safe distance away and waited for the bang. The bottle finally exploded blowing out a couple of windows right out.

Mind you, Fred liked to think he was as knowledgeable as the rest of the lads, and he tried to say big words like them, but very rarely got them right. Teasingly we would ask him, "How's poor Mr Coombs then, Fred?" waiting for him to say, "You know he's had his leg *amplicated*," and we would snigger and laugh at him behind our hands.

"And how's your Mother, Fred, still afraid to go out at nights, is she?"

"Well, 'tis like this yu see, 'er reads all them dreadful things in the *News of the World* and then 'ers frit to go out, 'er won't even go up the garden to the lavatory on her own in case 'ers *attached* by one a they *sectional* maniacs."

Once, when we were teasing Fred, our Mother came along and caught us, and didn't we get a hiding. "The trouble with you kids," our eldest brother said, as we licked our wounds, "is that you wants to learn the eleventh commandment and stick to it. Do you know what tis?" he asked us. "Thou shalt not be found out. The trouble is," he went on, "you be as green as grass, but get another few years behind you, and you'll learn." And we did, in time.

Mind you, young Ben seemed to be able to get away with mur-der. He was a jolly good mimic, too, and able to take anyone off.

And once when we were in chapel and the congregation were singing, with feeling, "Wash me in the Blood of the Lamb. And I
shall be whiter than snow", a tittering rose above the fine singing.
There was Ben taking off one of the visiting lay preachers, one
who always shut his eyes when he was singing and rocked backwards and forwards on his heels as he sang. And to add insult to
injury Ben was also singing a parody to the hymn:

> Whiter than the whitewash on the wall
> Whiter than the whitewash on the wall,
> Wash me in the water
> That you washed your dirty daughter
> And I shall be whiter than snow

We tried to shush him, but he was that full of himself he just
kept on. The audience gradually stopped the singing and Ben was
left carolling on his own. Then he looked round sheepishly and
burst out laughing.

We were banned from chapel after that. You see we were really
church, so the chapel was not actually turning away lost souls
and they knew it. But our Mother went down the village and
apologized to Mr Ivings who was one of the preachers at the
chapel, for Ben's shocking behaviour.

# 7

# Caravans and Kings

Living in Little Ducklington, just a few hundred yards away from us was Mr and Mrs Jesse Pratley. Their home was a brightly painted caravan which stood in a field next to the entrance to the moors. I do not know if they were of gipsy origin, but they were both dark and gypsy-like in their looks and dress. He was a big, black-eyed, swarthy type and she was small with jet-black curly hair and sloe-black eyes, and she dressed in the fashion of a gypsy too, with her long, black skirt and blouse and a black, shiny, sateen-like apron, and she had ear-rings of half-sovereigns in her pierced ears.

Mr Pratley always wore a red, spotted kerchief knotted round his neck, with the ends neatly tied to his braces.

The caravan was always neat and tidy, with its bed at the far end wideways across the van. It had on it a pink, rose-covered quilt, which was covered over by a beautiful hand crocheted lacy bedspread; the small table also had a white, lace-edge cloth on it. All this handwork was done by Mrs Pratley, she used to crochet her own shawls too. There was brass and copper in the caravan in the shape of water carriers, lamps and ornaments.

Mr Pratley was a coal and wood merchant and most days he would journey up to Witney Railway goods yard and load his cart with hundredweight sacks of coal, which he sold, not just to Ducklington housewives, but to many of the surrounding villages. His pony, at least the only one I can remember, was called Nora, and she had hindquarters like a cow.

When trees were being felled in the area, Jesse would buy

the tree top wood, leaving the trunk for the timber mer-
chants.

Sometimes our step-father would go along to the field and help
Jesse cut up the wood into blocks. He had a wonderful mechanical
saw which sawed through the timber in no time. Mr Pratley did
not pay our step-father, but he would often give him a big sack
of blocks which he carried home on his shoulder.

One Saturday afternoon he had gone along to give Jesse a hand,
and from our house we could hear the whine as the saw blade cut
through the wood. Suddenly our step-father came stumbling into
the house clutching his hand to his chest. He had Jesse's old red
kerchief wrapped round his left hand, which was supported by the
right one, blood dripping through his fingers onto the ground.

Betty, who was about eighteen at the time, rushed towards him.
"Whatever have you done?" she cried.

"Cut me bloody fingers awf I reckon," he said, wincing as he
did so.

Carefully she took off the blood-soaked kerchief. The top of one
of his fingers was all but off—it looked just like the lid of a
hinged salt cellar, she told us afterwards. And the other finger
was very badly cut too. She plunged his hand into a bowl of water
laced with Jeyes fluid. Our step-father, a very strong man, nearly
passed out with the pain. Quickly our Mother ripped up an old
sheet, handing Betty a piece so that she could swabble the injured
fingers. When she was sure that all the blood and dirt was washed
from the wounds, she started to try to bandage the fingers. She
said afterwards that she had, in fact, replaced the finger tip which
was completely severed, and the guides on the other one were cut.
She bound the two fingers, first separately and then both together,
which helped to keep them stiff.

In the middle of all the chaos of sheet tearing and water boiling and general confusion, Mrs Pratley came running down from
the caravan. She burst into the house crying, "I never ast
him to do it, I never ast him to do it." This was in case our
step-father claimed off them for injury, which of course he did not.

The author's mother when she was twenty

Ben Butler (*right*), the author's stepfather, beside the brewery's steam Sentinel lorry

The author (*second from right in second front row*) whilst attending St Mary's school, Witney

He never even went to the doctor for that would have meant that he would have to go on the panel, which in turn would have meant much less money for us to live on. The accident happened on the Saturday afternoon, but he went off to work as usual on the following Monday, with both fingers still strapped together. He must have been in pretty good fettle, and Betty must have made a very good job of doctoring him because his fingers healed in no time. One, of course, was permanently stiff and the other had a complete ring round the top where the flesh had healed and where Betty had stuck the fingertip back on.

Once, when Mr Pratley was out delivering coal, during a very hot, dry spell, one of the iron rims from one of the cart wheels came off. He was a long way from home, and from a blacksmith, and at first he thought that he would have to drive home without a rim on, which would have been bad for the wooden wheel as the rough roads would have soon cut into it. And Jesse knew that if he wore too much of the wood away, the wheel then would be completely spoilt. So he took hold of a thick rope which he kept in the cart, in case he needed a tow at any time, and wound it round and round the wheel. We heard him coming up the street that night, clump, clump, clump, the old cart went. Jesse said afterwards, "It nearly shook me guts out, 'twas worse than a ride on the cakewalk—and it lasted longer."

But back home Jesse soon put his cart to rights. He always had a spare wheel soaking in the water in the ditch that ran alongside the field where the caravan was. Mind you, they did not always match up. When Jesse was a bit pushed, he would fix a wheel on one side of his cart that was bigger than the other side, and this would cause a peculiar noise as he drove down the street. But in those days nobody took much notice of simple things like that.

It was Jesse Pratley who sent me on an errand one day, to get two pennoth of hurdle seed. Green as grass I made my way to the village shop, clutching the tuppence tightly in my hand. I was just about to open the shop door when I heard someone calling my name over and over again. I turned to see Mrs Pratley running

E

down the street after me. She came up to me, put her arm round me and told me that it was just a joke and Mr Pratley was only teasing me. "But you have that tuppence and spend it on some sweets, my little love," she cried. "That'll teach him not to send little girls on fools' errands."

I went into the shop. The joy of having tuppence to spend on what *I* wanted was unbelievable. It took me ages to make up my mind. First I thought I would have a sherbet fountain and a gob-stopper and some bulls' eyes, then I decided on some marzipan teacakes and some slab toffee and a halfpenny worth of bright yellow lemonade powder. Poor Mrs Tidball, who kept the shop, lost her usual patience.

"Why not have some of these?" she suggested, pointing to a jar of brightly coloured sweets.

"No, I don't want none of them," I replied. "Our Bet had some last week, they makes yu pee green."

So I settled for some Blue Bird toffees, a liquorish pipe and a sherbet dab.

Mrs Pratley used to accompany her husband round some of the remote Oxfordshire villages. While he was busy selling coal and logs, she would go off calling at the cottages with her wicker basket over her arm. It was filled with all the little odds and ends that the housewife needed, boot and shoelaces, collar studs, needles and pins, hair combs, hair pins, knots of tape and ribbon, elastic and clothes pegs, which she and her husband used to make. They would sit outside the caravan in the evenings, he whittling away skinning the wood and shaping the sticks while she expertly fixed the small tin band on to the top end of the peg, which kept it together.

Later on, when things got a bit better for them, Mrs Pratley acquired a pony and trap of her own, so that she could come and go when and where she wanted to. She also collected rags and rabbit skins as well as selling her wares, and sometimes our Mother would let me go with her. Mind you, I was not allowed to go with Mrs Pratley as she went from door to door. I used to have to sit on the cart and wait for her. "You just sit and guard them rags, young Mollie, see as nobody pinches um."

Often village children would come along and stare at me, sat there in all my glory. "You be a gippo," they would call to me. "You be a gippo, that's what you be."

"I ent then," I would cry. "I ent a gippo, I be just looking after these rags."

Then they would run off laughing and calling, " 'er's looking after they rags, 'er's a gippo."

And I would poke my tongue out at them and call back, "Sticks and stones will break my bones but names will never hurt me."

I was very fond of both Mr and Mrs Pratley and as a child spent many happy hours sitting on the steps of their caravan, while they made clothes pegs for the next day's journey.

I think Mrs Pratley must have had the gift of second sight, because she used to tell me about some of the ghostly things that she used to see, especially in the Minster Lovell area. That village was usually her last call of the day, after she had been round Astall, Swinbrook and Leafield. Well, one autumn evening she said it was getting a bit dimpsy and the mist was already lying low over the water meadows, shrouding the village in a mysterious veil, when suddenly a figure of a white knight rose up in front of her. He was dressed in shining armour and he was astride a huge white charger. Her pony shied, pulling the trap onto the side of the road. In a flash the rider and horse disappeared into the mist. She said she even saw the white breath coming from the animal's nostrils and his long, white tail was stretched out behind him.

It was years afterwards, when I was in my teens in fact, that I heard about the legend of Lord Francis Lovell, one of King Richard III's favourites. But when the King was killed at the battle of Bosworth, Lord Lovell knew that the King's enemies would seek him out and kill him, so he fled from the battlefield. Later, however, he took part in another battle and this time he fought for Lambert Simnel, a man who claimed to be Richard, Earl of Warwick and therefore lawful King of England. But King

Henry VII's men were too good for them, and Lord Lovell, reflecting on the outcome of the battle, left, and the story goes that he was last seen swimming his horse across the river Trent, but owing to the steepness of the opposite bank, was unable to land.

But the story goes that Lord Francis Lovell, now a hunted fugitive, managed to get back to the great Manor House at Minster Lovell, the home of the Lovell family, and with the help of a trusty manservant remained there, hidden in a secret room. The servant brought food and drink to his master daily but locked him in the secret room every night. Years passed and the story was regarded as just a legend. But in the year 1708 some workmen were engaged in repairing the manor, and behind a great chimney stack they made a startling discovery. Hidden in a small secret room they found the skeleton of a man seated at a table, with the skeleton of a small dog sitting at his feet. Was this the remains of Lord Lovell? Did his trusty servant die suddenly leaving his master entombed, to die of starvation?

Or was the ghost of the white knight that Mrs Pratley saw that of Lord Lovell trying in vain to reach the safety of his home. Whoever it was Mrs Pratley told me that she saw the same ghost on several occasions along the same stretch of road, but not necessarily in the same place.

And another 'sighting' of hers was that of Old Mother Culpepper, the ghost of a very old lady dressed all in black, with a little poked bonnet on her head, who walked along the tops of the hedges in the Hanborough area. Mrs Pratley used to tell me that as she jogged along in her pony and trap, Mrs Culpepper used to keep up with her until she reached a certain field and then the old lady would disappear as mysteriously as she had appeared.

Years later, during the Second World War, I heard of another 'sighting' of Old Mother Culpepper.

Many people were evacuated to this part of the country, from London, and one family, a mother and her three children, two girls aged twelve and ten and a boy of eight, lived in one of the villages near to Hanborough. The mother used to take the children back to

London at the weekends to see their father who had to stay in the city and work. They used to come back on the last train, so that it was around midnight when they reached Hanborough station, and they still had a matter of two miles to walk. They took a well-known short cut along a narrow lane. When they reached the cottage where they lived, on this particular evening the young boy was in a state of shock, white and trembling and he could not speak. The doctor was sent for and he said that the boy must have had a terrific shock to be in the state that he was. When the lad began to recover his mother asked him what had frightened him, and the boy replied, "It was that queer old lady dressed all in black that walked along the hedge all the way up the lane with us." Only then did the locals tell them about the ghost of Old Mother Culpepper. But it was only the young lad who had seen her.

# 8

# Poaching Tales and Tall Stories

"I be just goin' to take the cows down to the long field," Fred Paver used to say. A stranger hearing him make this remark would naturally think that he was really going to do this. But we in Ducklington knew darned well that what old Fred meant was, that he was about to take his cows down the road, round Starlum as we called it, from Ducklington to Curbridge, a matter of two miles. Here, along the grass verges he grazed his herd of six cows once every day, and this was what he called "the long field". Fred only had a couple of small fields so he found this free grazing a godsend. Goodness only knows how he made a living for after he had milked his cows he spent the rest of the day strolling leisurely along the road with the cows. Of course there was so little traffic about in those days, especially round the Curtbridge road. He used to meet a few village people on the way. For most every day wet or fine, poor lame Dick Clarke would be hobbling out for a walk, and he was always glad when folks stopped to have a few words with him. And Fred used to tell the tale that one day a man in a motor car stopped and called out to him, "I say, do you locals call the town I've just come through Cirencester or Sisister?" "Well sir," Fred replied, "we generally calls it Witney."

Fred would often meet Brummy Edward too, not that Brummy wasted much time chatting. If he was not laying a hedge or doing a bit of ditching for a farmer, he would be working away on his allotments. He had two at Ducklington and one in the next village at Curbridge. Sometimes he walked there, over the fields and footpaths, which was a more direct way than the roadway. Someone once asked Brummy why he kept two allotments in the village and another one at Curbridge and his reply was, "If I didn't grow plenty of vegetables my children would be no bigger than field mice." As well as cultivating the allotments, Brummy, like many of the village people at that time, used to do a bit of poaching on the side. His keen eyes knew just where the rabbit and hare runs were, and he would set his snares just where the animals made a habit of coming through a hedge or ditch.

As well as setting traps and snares to catch game, he also kept a couple of whippit-type dogs: one used to run along the grass verges while the other sat alongside Brummy in his little cart. He had a whistle hung round his neck, which he blew when he wanted the dogs to "go", "fetch" or "bring". He had trained them just as a shepherd might train a sheepdog.

The dog which was running would flush out the game and the one on the cart would take a flying leap and bring the bounty back to his master. Brummy's cart was pulled by a mule which he had bred himself, from a he-ass and a mare. In later years when most of his family had grown up and left home, Brummy used to plant the whole of one of his allotments with broad beans which he fed to his old mule by the bucketful.

One day Brummy had been helping with the harvest on one of the nearby farms, and at midday the farmer brought out some home-made cider for the men. A visiting farmer rode into the yard just as Brummy was taking a swig from the jar. "What's the cider like today then Brummy?" he enquired. And Brummy, the wise old man that he was replied, "If it was any worse, I couldn't drink it, and if it was any better I shouldn't have the chance!"

I really do not know how some of the families in the village would have managed to survive in those days without a bit of poaching. And although our Mother did not encourage Bern or Bunt to go, she was really quite glad when Denis, the youngest, took it up. He would come back from his escapades with wild ducks, rabbits and hares and sometimes a pheasant. But she was always uneasy in case he should get caught. When you had got a large hungry family and no money in your purse, you cooked your ill-gotten gains with a song in your heart, but with a prayer on your lips.

One day my eldest brothers Bern and Bunt were over on our allotment digging up the potatoes, when they noticed a man who lived in the village creeping up the side of the hedge in one of Farmer Strange's fields.

"I'll bet that old sod's setting a rabbit trap; we'll go and see when he's gone home," Bunt said. So they hid behind the huge trunk of one of Druce's elm trees and waited there until the man made off towards the village. Then they both walked over to where he had been crouching. After a bit of searching they found the snare the fellow had cunningly set across a hare run, and decided that they would tell nobody about it but, they would get up early the next morning to see if there was anything caught in it.

They crept out of the house at half-past five in the morning, across the green and up the Curbridge road they went, cutting across Druce's field and into Strange's to where the snare was set. In it was a beautiful hare, dead of course. Very carefully they lifted the body out and re-set the trap, in hopes that the man would never know that it had been tampered with. Then they cut off home as fast as their legs would carry them. Our Mother was amazed to see the boys coming through the gate carrying a sack at that time in the morning.

"Guess what we've got?" Bunt asked her excitedly. Then Bern thrust his hand into the sack and brought out the lovely, sandy-haired, long-eared hare. He held it at arm's length and it was nearly as big as he.

Our Mother gave a loud whoop of joy which was probably heard a quarter of a mile away. "Where on earth did you get that?" she cried, almost beside herself with excitement.

Bern and Bunt, both talking at the same time, told her how they had watched the man the day before, then found where he had set the trap, and how they sneaked off before anyone was up to see what was caught in it.

"Well," she said, "I'd best get it skinned just as quick as I can, then I'll put it to soak in some salt water for a while, and cook it for tea tonight. We'll have it jugged," she gabbled on. "I'll cook it in that big brown stone jar that belonged to Granny Broad, and then we will all sit down tonight and have a meal fit for a king. Let me see," she went on, "if I can get it in that old fire oven by eleven o'clock, that will have seven hours slow cooking. When you have had your breakfast, one of you can pop up to Mrs Adams and ask her for three or four bay leaves, jugged hare 'ent nothing without a few bay leaves in."

She made the boys some porridge, then went out into the back kitchen and started to skin the hare. She had not been out there very long when there was a loud banging on the door. She went to answer it, wiping her bloody hands on her coarse apron as she went.

The man who had set the trap stood there, his eyes blazing with temper. "Oh yes," he shouted eyeing her blood stained hands, "Oh yes, it *was* your Bern and Bunt that stole my hare, wasn't it? I followed thur tracks in the wet grass you see Missus, come on, it's no good trying to deny it; 'and it over quick, or I'll go and fetch the police."

"You'll go and do what?" our Mother shouted indignantly. "You'll go and do what?"

"I'll go up to Witney, thas what I'll do and fetch a policeman," he bellowed.

"Go on then, fetch one if you dare," our Mother cried, "you haven't got permission from Mr Strange to set snares in his field. We've got just as much right to the hare as you, you'd be frightened to death to go anywhere near the police station, they'd soon put you inside with your reputation. Go on, clear off with you," she went on, "and I hope Bern and Bunt finds some more of your traps that you've set, and don't you dare let me hear that you've said anything to my boys about this either, or you'll have me to answer to."

"You haven't heard the last of this," he shouted as he stamped out of the yard. "I'll get my own back one of these days, you mark my words if I don't."

Of course he knew that legally he had not got a leg to stand on and, as far as we knew, he never told another soul about the incident.

He knew that our Mother was a lot more knowledgeable than he was, and what she had said was right. Had the affair happened to a simpler sort of person, he would have probably bullied them into handing over the animal.

In those hard-up days there was much rivalry between the men who did a bit of poaching; everyone knew that it went on, and occasionally a landowner would take some poor devil to court, having been caught with pheasants on him. But hungry men with hungry families grew very cunning and very rarely got caught. And once when Shirty Calcutt and another local man called Denole started arguing about the ownership of a rabbit which had been caught in a trap, the local policeman acted as referee when they decided to fight each other for the rabbit.

"Righto, off you go," the policeman said. "And remember the winner takes the rabbit," and at once the two men fell upon each other, fighting and wrestling and rolling over in the road. They fought for nearly an hour, tearing at each other like mad things. When both of the men were absolutely exhausted, the policeman said, "Well, I declare the result of this fight a draw, so I'll take the rabbit," and he promptly got on his bicycle and rode away, leaving the men speechless.

Not only did we feed off the fat of the land, but from the rivers too. Proper fishing tackle was unheard of, so the lads of the village used to use their own methods to catch fish. They would cut themselves a good long withy stick and fix a rabbit wire on the end of it. Mind you, you also needed a steady hand, and a good eye to be able to see the fish laying on the bottom of the river. Then all you had to do was slip the wire over the fish's head, then give a sharp tug and yank it out of the water. Our Mother was not all that keen on fresh water fish, but she used to jolly them up with herbs and things and it used to make quite a tasty dish.

Some of the older men could even catch fish with their hands. You needed the patience of a saint, lying there on your stomach with your hand in the water waiting for a fish to come along and settle, before you began to tiggle its stomach. Crayfishing was a very popular sport too; crayfish bred well in our limestone river. And I remember once our cousins, who also lived in Ducklington, Harry Del and Pete Woodley, had been crayfishing one evening and they had caught dozens and dozens of the little fellows. But their parents were cross with them because they were late getting home and said that they would not cook them that night, but they would have to wait until the next day. So they put the live crayfish (they have to be cooked alive) in a bucket of water and stood them in the larder. When their father, our Uncle Harry, got up the next morning the crayfish had all disappeared. Apparently they had crawled out of the full backet and were all over the house, in the furniture, in the ashes that were left in the firegrate, even in the coalbox. So the boys did not have their treat after all, because most of the crayfish were dead, as they can only live a certain time out of fresh water.

I suppose you could call egg pinching sort of poaching too. I mean pheasant, partridge and duck eggs all of which our boys used to find and bring home. And one day a gang of the village lads were walking in the plantations at Cokethorpe and one of the Godfrey boys stumbled on a pheasant's nest absolutely full of eggs. At once he threw his great arms around the nest, shouting "They're mine, they're mine, none of you others 'ent going to have any of 'um." The rest of the lads crowded round protesting loudly when a stern voice over the other side of the hedge said, "Whose eggs did you say they were?" It was the voice of the head-keeper. Scared out of their wits the lads all took to their heels and ran home as if Old Nick was after them.

And a man who farmed at Coursehill, which was about a mile from Ducklington, had his suspicions that there was a fair bit of rabbit poaching going on on his land, but he could not seem to catch the culprits. Night after night he lay in wait at different places around the farm, at points where he thought they might enter his fields. Then one evening he was just making for home when he heard voices coming from the Great Western Railway line which skirted his land. The poachers were just off home—to Witney—and he had been thinking all along that the men netting his rabbits had come from Ducklington.

The next night he let the men come into the fields and saw them creeping along the hedges, frightening the rabbits and sending them into the long nets, from which, once they were in, there was no escape: Then one of the men said, "All right, pass the word along, thas enough for one night."

Then the farmer stood up and shouted, "All right fellows, we've got 'um." making out that he had plenty of help. "Come on," he went on, shouting at the poachers, "come on out you thieving buggers, there's more of us than there is of you." But no one came out; the poachers must have shot off in all directions back to Witney, leaving their long nets full of rabbits. The farmer collected them up, and the next morning took three sacks of rabbits into White's shop in Oxford, and got ninepence a-piece for them.

Another story of poaching that is told around Ducklington happened at the beginning of six weeks' terribly hard weather. The tale is about two men who had come to live in one of the nearby villages, town fellows they were. They had heard the locals talking about their poaching conquests, so they thought that they would have a go at it. It did not seem that difficult, and they might get a few good meals out of it. So without telling anyone of their plans, they set off. One of the men had a motor-bike and sidecar, they would go on this, but leave it at a fair distance away from where they hoped to catch, or rather, pick off the branches, some roosting pheasants. It was a freezing cold night and trying to snow as the men made their way down to the wood. But nothing went the way they planned: the men, not used to creeping about woods in the dark, made far too much noise as they trod on rotten wood, which snapped and crackled in the quiet air. Suddenly someone shouted, "All right, I've got you covered, walk towards the sound of my voice with your hands above your head, or I'll blast your bloody legs from under you." Both men turned and fled, running for their lives, stumbling and falling, as they tripped over fallen trees. At last they emerged from the wood, breathless and bleeding where they had run blindly into brambles and branches. They reached the safety of the motor-bike, and Bill the driver threw himself on the machine and started it up, while Fred jumped on to the top of the sidecar, where he sat perched, too breathless to get right in.

Their journey home took them through Ducklington, and they tore round by the pond at a rare pace and then on up towards the Aston Hills towards home. Bill pulled up at the house where Fred his passenger lived, and said, "All right, mate, 'op out quick, and make yourself scarce," but there was no reply, because there was no one in the sidecar. Bill was worried sick about his mate, but he dare not go looking for him in case he ran into the keeper. Well, Fred did not turn up the next day, or the next, so the police were notified, and a lot of questions were asked but they still could not find out what had happened to him.

Now the story goes that when Bill was driving home that night and was rounding the pond at Ducklington at speed, Fred, who was still only perched on the top of the sidecar, rolled off, striking his head on the road as he fell, rolling into the pond as he did so. The terrible hard frost that night froze the pond over solid, and the severe weather lasted for six long weeks, and it was only when the thaw came that Fred's body was found.

But there were many different ways of eking out a living. One old fellow who did not seem to do anything else in the way of work, used to make walking sticks from ash wood, cutting the straight sticks low at the base from where they were growing, and here, there was always a sort of knobble. He used to carve dog's faces on this knobbly piece which also formed the handle of the walking stick. Then he would take them up to Witney and get one of the barbers to sell them to his customers when they came in for a hair cut.

Even the choir boys used to earn themselves a bit of pocket money now and then. Once our rector, the Rev. Tristram, thought he would get the boys to clear the weed plantain from the church-yard. He offered the choir boys a penny a dozen for all the roots they brought him. He even got Mr Barratt the village blacksmith to make each boy a special little two-pronged tool, which helped to lift the long rooted weed out of the ground. All went well, the boys were doing fine, earning themselves quite a lot of pocket money. But after a few weeks, the rector realized that the weeds in the churchyard were not getting less. Then he discovered, that after he had carefully counted out the plantain roots, and paid over the money, and told his gardener to tip them on the rubbish heap at the bottom of the rectory garden, the choir boys were simply picking them off the heap and offering them again to the Rector for payment.

# 9

## Come Day, Go Day, God send Sunday

Sometimes in the summer time there was a bit of excitement in the village when some of the farmers' hayricks caught on fire. Because, if the grass had not been allowed to dry and make good hay, the ricks were inclined to 'heat', often with disastrous results. If a farmer spotted a rick steaming he would ask a couple of his men to try and cut the offending hay out, and it was nothing to see a two or more farmer workers, stripped to the waist, cutting away at the centre of a rick with a huge hay knife. They would throw the damp hay out on to the grass below where the cows soon ate it up. When they were sure that the danger of fire was past, they would emerge from the rick looking like fugitives from a minstrel concert party.

But sometimes the ricks were left too long 'heating' and that would cause them to set on fire. The only thing left then was to send for the Fire Brigade.

I remember winter mornings too, waking up to hear the great lumbering threshing tackle going by, puffing and snorting its way down the village street, to set up at Wilsdon's or Strange's farms. They would be in the village for a week or more threshing the corn ricks and puffing chaff and coal smoke all over the place. The men, swarthy and strong, mostly wore navy blue boiler suits, and their faces were as black as tinkers from the dust which came from the cornricks. From any part of the village you could hear the engine that drove the threshing machine, start up at about seven

o'clock in the mornings and it went on all day until half-past four
or five o'clock at night. We used to stop and watch the men at
work, when we came out of school.

"Stand well back, you children," the farmer would shout to us,
"unless you wants your head 'ett off with a rat."

When they had nearly reached the bottom of a rick, the big boys
and the farmer would stand round it with stout sticks in their
hands, because this was when the rats, who had been living happily
in the ricks since harvest time, made a run for their lives. As they
ran out the waiting boys whacked them on the head and killed
them; the few they missed the dogs made short work of.

Another thing I remember about the winter times of our young
days in Ducklington, was when my elder brothers Bern and Bunt
used to go beating for the local farmers and gentry. The boys
started to go beating when they were about thirteen. Sometimes on
a Friday Mr Salmon, one of the head gamekeepers, used to go into
the school and ask the headmaster if he would enquire if any of
the older boys would like to go beating the next day. Of course
nearly all the lads said yes, because it meant they would get a
shilling, a good midday dinner and a rabbit for their day's work.

Later on, when they were older, my brothers used to receive two
shillings and sixpence and a good dinner and a rabbit. This was in
the days before wellington boots, and the only protection against
the wet and mud was a pair of strong, leather boots and putties.
Most men and boys wore these putties, a remnant from the First
World War. You could purchase them from Cook & Boggis's shop
in Witney for threepence a pair, but I expect the ones Bern and
Bunt wore were some that our step-father had himself worn during the 1914–18 war. Mind you, there were lads who had not even
got putties to wear because they could not afford to buy any, then
old sacking was wound round and round the legs to try and stave
off some of the wet.

The variation of the midday meal that the beaters had depended
on which farmer they were working for. At one place they had
lashings of rabbit pie, great big ones they were, made in huge

cream pans, about two foot across oozing with meat and lovely thick, brown gravy, topped up with potatoes and greens, with a great big slab of bread and butter pudding for afters and as much cocoa as you wanted. At another farm a bucketful of stew and chunks of bread was brought into the room where the men and boys had their food, they were handed basins and spoons and simply helped themselves to as much stew as they could manage. And at another they had super beef sandwiches and a mug of hot soup.

At one of the places they went to, Brummy Edwards was in charge of the beaters. He was a wise old fellow and taught my brothers quite a few wrinkles about beating. "You go and poke they brambles," Brummy would say, "I'll bet thurs a rabbit in thur," and sure enough two or three rabbits would rush out. "You lay one a they in the ditch, my lad," he said to Bern one day, who was struggling along with three or four hares. "You can always come back fer him tomorrow."

So Bern did this on several occasions, but sometimes the hare that he had carefully hidden was gone, already found by someone else. And one day Bunt acquired an extra rabbit. In the early afternoon they were beating through a small spinney when a couple of rabbits ran out. Someone took a shot at them and killed one. Nobody wanted to start loading themselves up with game that early in the afternoon, so Bunt threw the dead rabbit in the hedge, thinking that he could pick it up for the farmer when they all made their way back to the farm at night. Somehow the rabbit was forgotten. At the end of the day the men and boys lined up for their pay and a rabbit, and only then did Bunt remember the one in the hedge. Later when he was walking home along with Bern and a fellow called Skeecher, Bunt made out that he wanted to go to the lavatory and that he would catch them up. In a few minutes he found the rabbit, tied its legs with string, let the rabbit down inside his trouser leg then tied the string to his braces. He ran and caught Bern and Skeecher up. Of course neither of them realized what he had got, and he did not let on until Bern and he

F

were safely indoors. There was great jubilation in our house that night. We were rich, we had three rabbits and an extra five shilling that the boys had earned. "I wouldn't call the King me aunt," our Mother remarked happily. This was a favourite expression of hers when she was very pleased about something.

A great event in our lives was when you got hold of *two* two-pound golden syrup tins and a fair piece of string; then you could set about making yourself a pair of stilts. You see golden syrup was a luxury in our house so you had to wait ages before you got two tins. Besides that, you had to take your turn with the rest of the family. But once you had got your tins all you had to do was to turn them upside down and pierce two holes in each tin, in the bottom sides opposite each other. You didn't need a lid. After cutting the string in two, one for each stilt, you simply pushed one end of the string through one hole and tied a knot in the end, so that it would not pull through the hole. This knot must be on the inside of the tin, and then you would poke the other end of the string in the other hole and tie the end in a knot just as you did the other side. This gave you a loop of string which acted as a sort of rein. So now the original bottom of the tin was the top of your stilt. To use them you simply placed your feet on the top of the tins, then you just lifted the string up and down as you walked along.

"You looks as 'ockered as a pig in pattens," Dick Clarke called to me when I met him down the village as I hobbled along on my newly acquired stilts.

Dick was always glad when anyone stopped to have a chatter to him. Being a cripple he did not get much further than just up and down the village street a little way, and that was quite an effort for him. But he nearly always had a little tale to tell or a bit of village gossip.

"Have you heard the story about the milestone inspector (tramp) that called at Witney workhouse one day then, young Mollie?"

"No," I said, glad to slip my feet from the stilts and sit down on the dirt path for a rest.

"Well," Dick said, "this is supposed to be gospel truth and I'm relaying it just as I heard it. One cold night a man was admitted to the Witney workhouse, but the only place they could find for him to sleep was in the mortuary. Not very inviting and perishing cold, and thur was already a corpse thur in an open coffin. After looking round, the man decided that the warmest place (in the burra) would be in the coffin, so he moved the corpse onto the bench he had been given, and got in. In the morning somebody came in with his breakfast, and tried without success to rouse the corpse. The man watched this for a minute and then sitting up slowly in the coffin and said, 'Well if 'e won't 'ett it I 'ull.' The attendant fled from the room frightened out of his wits."

"That 'ent true is it, Dick?" I asked, as we laughed over his story.

"Of course it is," he replied, "coo, I'll bet he wasent half cold staying the night in that old morgue, I should think the only place he sweat was at the nose end. Which is more than can be said about I," Dick went on. "I be maggled to death, I be that sweaty."

I expect it was the fact that Dick could not walk without the aid of two walking sticks; even so he could only just shuffle along, and it was indeed a beautiful day. The hot sun bore down on us as we made our way slowly down the road. Then we stopped to lean on Holton's wall and watched the shepherd at work while Dick got his breath back.

The shepherd was busy rubbing something into the sheeps' woolly backs.

"What's up with 'um?" Dick enquired.

"Ah, they got the maggot summut dreadful," he replied. "I've had to treat every one of 'um, but this is some pretty good stuff as I rubs into 'um. I done some of the sheep 'issday (yesterday) and within a couple of hours they maggots was fallin' out like rice through a cullendar, so I've done the rest today. Course the gaffer was a bit upset about it, but I told 'im it was nothin' to get upstrapluss about, wus things 'appens at sea."

"Ah!" Dick said, "I got summut to ask you. Now a man was telling I that on the farm wur he works they always puts some geese and a gander in the same field wur the sheep be lambing, to keep the foxes away, cos one year the farmer lost a lot of his lambs, that old fox used to pick um up like picking up stones. Did you ever hear of anybody doing that before?" Dick asked him.

"Ah, I have hear tell as folks does that, they do say the geese and ganders in a farmyard be as good as a dog any day."

"Ah," Dick went on. "What about all they flies as we've been plagued with fer weeks. I hopes they'll soon get shot of um. They do say as a council man from Witney come to Ducklington yesday and had a talk about um with Frankie the chairman of the parish council. Course they goes and sends a lad-di-dah chap, the sort as don't understand our lingo. Because when this man said to Frankie 'What sort of flies are they?" and Frankie replied, 'Ah, they be they blue *asst uns*,' and this yer fellow ses 'Do you mean to tell me that this plague of flies you've got in Ducklington come from *Aston*?' " (A village two miles away.)

Then Dick got on to a more serious subject.

"Did you hear what happened to 'bomber Claridge' then, damn near got hisself killed he did. He was jogging along with his old horse and cart on his way to Witney. And you knows that horse is usually as quiet as a lamb, well, summut must have upset him cos all of a sudden he pricked up his ears and took off up that road like a wild thing. It took old Bomber by surprise and as the horse bolted the reins was flung out of his hands, then the cart hit the grass verge and over the lot went into the ditch with poor old Bomber underneath the lot. Well, 'twas your Uncle Harry, Mollie, as see it all 'appening as he was coming home from work on his bike. With his body he eased the cart up so as he could get to Bomber who had got all the reins sort of wound round his body. He gets out his pocket knife and cut the leather reins and dragged old Bomber out, wet as a toad he was, and the first words that the ungrateful old beggar said was, 'Now I shall have to buy some new reins'."

Leaving Dick and the old shepherd still chattering, I mounted my stilts and went on my way further down the village.

First I met Sally Saunders; she had her hair done up in rag curlers, like a heap of conkers her head looked and I told her so.

"Ah, you be only jealous," she replied, "cos you haven't got nothing new to wear at Whitsun (Whitsunday was in fact the next day). You know what they ses if you 'ent got nothing new fer Whitsun don't you?" She went on, "They ses the birds 'ull shit on you, ha ha they'll shit on you all right," she shouted as she ran indoors.

Then I made my way down to Gooseham by the river. In a field down there that backed on to one of the farms were some stone buildings, where Mick and Ben and some of the other kids had built themselves a den. They had pulled one or two of the stones from the side of one of the smaller buildings and poked elder branches to make a sort of roof, then pushed some on the ground for the upright of their den. It was quite big inside and they were having great fun. It was their sort of summer camp, with large stones that they had found acting as stools. Apparently they had just been reinforcing the roof and young Ben, who was about nine at the time, was sitting inside. Suddenly the side of the building began to fall in and part of it came crashing down around Ben's ears. He crawled out of the rubble, miraculously not a stone had hit him, but he was crying and very frightened. We knew that our Mother would go mad if she found out. First of all the danger that Ben had been put in, and secondly to think that it was because they had been pulling stones from the building, that the side had caved in, and this was damaging the farmer's property.

We dared Ben and all the other kids that they were never to breathe a word to a soul. I forget what we threatened them with but it must have been pretty drastic, because no one ever knew a word about it. But for months, every night young Ben woke up in bed screaming and had awful nightmares, and our Mother could not understand what was causing them. Always there was something falling on him, Ben cried, but he never let on, and in time the nightmares ceased.

Even now when I open a tin of syrup I am back in the meadow on that hot summer day, my stilts slung over my shoulder because I could not walk on them in the grass. The acrid smell of bruised elder leaves and the dragonflies—we called them devil's darning needles, darting and flying over the river, and young Ben screaming and the other kids crying because they were frightened.

## *10*

# *Uncle Jesse and Pigsty Passion*

Uncle Jesse was not anybody's Uncle really, but all the children called him uncle. He lived in a hut at the far end of the village. A bit of a mystery was Uncle Jesse. No one really knew from where he had originated, but to me he always seemed to have lived in his hut. In fact when I grew up I found that he had come to settle in the village just after the First World War. He had a sort of nasal twang, picked up, we discovered, from his numerous visits to Canada.

He was a tall, bronzed, freckly man with sandy hair and a waxed military moustache and a distinct military bearing; he marched rather than walked, striding out, arms swinging, with a back as straight as a ramrod, and although his hut was small and cramped, he was always clean and tidy with a freshly sponged celluloid collar round his tanned neck—a striped shirt, khaki trousers and an army greatcoat.

He was a 'Jack of all trades' having the ability to do almost anything. He worked mostly on the farms in the neighbourhood, never at one for long, just 'jobbing' from one to the other. He could shear sheep quicker than anyone in the district, lay a hedge, or plough a furrow as straight as the next man. Engines he was very clever with, and when the first steam ploughs and tractors came grunting into the village Uncle Jesse was the only one who knew anything about them.

We were watching him repair an old threshing drum one day and he started to tell us about when he was in Canada.

"Thur ent no fields out there," he told us. "Well, not fields like we got here any road. One farmer would have acres and acres of land stretching as far as the eye could see, thur's no hedges, just miles and miles of golden corn, and at harvest time there might be anything up to eight horse-drawn binder machines working alongside one another. Then gradually most of the farmers bought steam ploughs and then tractors, which still pulled the old type cutters and binders behind us. My word, that was a sight too, a dozen or more tractors driving across the prairies, all in line, like an army on the move they looked, except that they was cutting thousands of acres of corn.

"Well, one scorching hot day twenty of us started work, ten driving tractors and the others sitting on the back of the binder where 'twas their job to see that each sheaf was tied and flung out in straight lines. We was getting on quite well when suddenly the tractor that was working next to we caught fire; the other drivers quickly drove theirs out of the way of the one that was burning—but then the corn caught fire, thur was a bit of a breeze a-blowing, and it looked as if the whole corn harvest for miles would be going up in flames.

"Quick as a flash I could see what I had to do. I shouted to Bert Atkins, my buddy, who was set on the binder at the back, 'Bert be you game, boy? Shall we try and cut round it?' 'Yes,' he hollered back, 'but get a move on before it all goes up like tinder.'

"So I drove round the outside of the spreading fire in a huge circle cutting the corn as we went. Round and round we drove sealing off the rest of the prairie. The other lads, seeing what we was doing, armed thurselves with anything they could lay hands on and began to beat out the fire that tried to spread on to the stubble. After half an hour the fire was out and old Bert and I was heroes— well, in the boss's eyes we was, we had saved the corn, with little more than four or five acres spoilt which was nothing really.

"Now go off home to tea, you kids," he said to us, "that's enough story-telling for today."

But if we knew that Uncle Jesse was working at any of the farms, we children would make a bee-line for the farmyard in the hope that we might see him. Sometimes it was too wet for him to work outside, then we would all make for one of the old barns where we would perch ourselves on straw bales and there we would sit, wide-eyed, listening to his tales of travel and excitement.

"How many times have you been over the water?" Jack Everet asked him one day.

"Oh, six er seven times," Uncle Jesse replied, "but I shan't be goin' no more now, me travelling days are over," he said. "I shall stay here till the good Lord calls me home to his golden acres in the sky."

"Tell us about the things you done when you was young, before you went to Canada," one of the boys said.

"Well, we was a big family," Uncle Jesse told us. "Ten of us, six boys and four gels, and my father was a farm labourer bringing home twenty-five shillings a week. So when we boys got older we used to go off poaching to get a bit of extra grub; worried our poor old mother to death it did. She knew as we would be sent to prison if we was caught—but we never was. Mind you we had some near goes I can tell you, and some damn good dinners too.

"Rabbits we could catch with a snare, and hares too sometimes. But it was them long-tailed uns (pheasants) as we liked to catch. Thur was several different ways of poaching um without the noise and expense of a gun.

"One way we used to do it was to get hold of some nice plump winey raisins; our mother made a lot of home-made wine you see. Well, we would fix one or two raisins on a fishing hook, using an old fishing line that our mother had bought for threepence from a jumble sale. Then we would lay the hook and line in the grass where we knew some pheasants usually fed. Then we would lie in the hedge holding the fishing line tightly, and wait for the birds to come along. Sure enough, they soon found the winey raisins and with a fish-hook down their throat they couldn't squawk— then before you could say 'Jack Robinson' we had their old necks wrung and they was stowed away in the sack.

"Back home, our Mother used to worry and grumble—she didn't know what to do with the feathers, somebody was sure to see um. So we carefully collected every one up and chucked them on the back of the fire—coo didn't they stink too! 'If anybody smells them feathers burning they'll know we be up to something,' our Mother would cry. 'Tell um you emptied your feather bed and what they smelt was the ones that you swept up afterwards,' our Father told her.

"But thur's more than one way of killing a cat," Uncle Jesse went on, "and pheasants too for that matter. Another way we used to catch um was by tying up some flowers of sulphur in a piece of flannel, tie the flannel on to a piece of wire and hang it up in a tree just underneath where we knew the birds roosted. Then we'd sit and wait till the pheasants had settled for the night, then we'd set fire to the flannel—talk about pong—the fumes was that strong the birds was soon overcome and would fall off the tree like ripe apples in autumn. Ah, we had more pheasants than you've had hot dinners," Uncle Jesse said, bragging a little.

"Ah, 'tis and ill wind as blows nobody good," he went on. "Take the flooding as we allus get in February, cos in my young days that month allus lived up to the saying 'February fill dyke', and although the village where we lived was very low-lying and some of the houses flooded summut dreadful, the rains brought some compensation. Our Mother would call us and say 'the floods be up boys', and when we looked out of the cottage window and saw the great expanse of water we knew 'twas time to go rabbit catching.

"You see, as the water gradually flooded the fields the rabbits would come out of their burrows and run up the withy trees, and sit there to keep dry, and thur they had to stay, trapped, either till the floods subsided or we went and grabbed 'um: 'twas as easy as picking cherries. Some days we've had as many as twenty rabbits; our Mother used to keep four or five for us, then we'd take a couple down the village and give to Ted Carter and his Missus— they was an old couple who was very poor and they loved to get hold of a rabbit or two. 'Best take one to your Auntie Florrie as well,' our Mother would say, 'not that she deserves one,' she would add, but we boys never asked why.

"The rest we sold cheaply to the folk in the village, giving our Mother the money. 'You're good boys to me,' she would say with tears in her eyes, 'I don't like to take it, but I must get Margie's boots mended for school on Monday.'

"Ah," Uncle Jesse went on, "and other times we used to get hold of the long-tailed un's, was either when we'd had a good sharp hoar frost or perhaps arter that had been snowing all night. Well, we lads would get up early and pick the roosting pheasants awf the trees like picking pears. You see, when they a-bin perching all night and the snow 'ad settled on 'um, specially on their tails, thur was no warmth to melt it, and then along would come Jack Frost and freeze that snow hard—well, in the morning, the poor devils couldn't take off. Mind you, if we hadn't bin up to all them sort of games we should never 'ave made it, grub was that short and money was shorter.

"Course a lot of the credit should go to our Mother, for the wonderful meals as 'er cooked fer us. I reckon her was just about the best cook in the world, talk about make your mouth water, I regler froths at the mouth just thinking of they lovely meals.

"Course the gentry in them days, well most of um anyroad, thought as everything belonged to them and that nobody else should have anything. The lord of the manor in our village was Lord Boverton, owned a lot of land he did. Well, he was out one morning, riding round his estate on his horse when he came to his boundary where his land joined a small farmer's few acres, and the small farmer whose name was Parker was very busy cutting and laying a hedge. 'Morning, squire,' Jack Parker said politely, 'Good morning, Parker,' his lordship replied, 'I'll bet you get hold of some of my pheasants when they stray on to your land don't you?' 'Well,' Parker replied, 'if they strays on to my land they byent yours any longer be 'um, and I take a perticular notice as they don't stray back neither.' "

"Uncle Jesse's mother used to put mushrooms in their rabbit pudding," I said to our Mother, after we had been listening to him telling us tales of his youth.

"Ah well, perhaps his mother hadn't got seven hungry mouths to feed like I have. Besides," she went on, "I never seems to find any mushrooms at the same time as I gets hold of rabbits and vice versa, and don't forget," she said, shouting at me, "no going out until you've cleaned the knives and forks." How I hated that chore, one which I had to do each week.

"I can't find the Monkey brand,"* I said, trying to get out of doing the job.

"There's none left and I got no money to buy any, you'll have to use elbow grease and ashes instead," she cried.

Young as I was I knew what she meant by using ashes, but elbow grease I had never heard of before. I searched around in the back kitchen, amongst the old rag dusters and half tins of brasso and boot polish that had gone hard because someone had left the lid off. Then Betty came in, "I can't find the elbow grease," I said, and she burst out laughing.

"She can't find the elbow grease," she cried going into the living-room, telling the rest of the family, and they all hooted with laughter and I burst out crying. Then Bunt came up to me.

"Don't take any notice of 'um, look this is elbow grease," he said, "just rubbing hard till you polishes it," and he started to clean the knives. "You just go and rout some fine ash from the grate and I'll help you." So we cleaned the knives and forks together, spitting first on the rag, then dipping it in the ash and then rubbing very hard, with 'elbow grease'. Mind you, we only thought that it worked with spit; no doubt plain water would have worked just as well. One of the knives still smelt violently of onions (our Mother had been peeling some for dinner) and they must have been rather strong.

* Monkey brand was a block of sort of solid vim; you simply rubbed knives and forks across it and it made them shiny. Of course, they were made of steel in those days.

"You'd better go and put him in the garden," Bunt said, "that'll start her off again if you don't." So I went outside and plunged the knife blade down into the earth several times, until all trace of the onion smell had gone. Then I wiped the knife, put it in the box with the others and was soon off out again. If our Mother was in a bad mood, the best thing was to keep well out of the way until whatever was causing it had passed. But mostly I think it was because half the time she did not know where the next shilling was coming from.

I went in search of Uncle Jesse, but could not find him. He had not seemed too well lately, he would tell us one story and then say "that's all for today you kids, I got a bit of a head, I shall have to go and lie down."

A few weeks later when we came home from school our Mother said, "They took Uncle Jesse away last night to Woodstock workhouse, he's pretty bad I think."

Two days later we heard that he had died, but I cannot remember what he died from. Poor old Uncle Jesse. He had fought for his country and had saved a prairie in Canada, and now he was gone. We children missed him and his cheery stories, but the rest of the villagers went on as if nothing had happened.

In my childhood the seasons seemed to dominate our lives. In winter we did not go far afield, perhaps into the next village or into town, but when the spring sunshine broke through and there were violets down the lane our Mother would say, "Ah, if 'tis like this come Saturday, we'll walk over to see Auntie May." She lived about four miles away in the next village but one to us and she and Uncle Patrick were distantly related to us. "Their cat walked across our garden," was the expression Mother used when people asked what the relationship to our family was.

But come Saturday, most likely the east wind was rushing down from Siberia or wherever it came from and the trip to Auntie May's would be put off time and time again.

Then we would wake up one morning to find that spring had really arrived, the air was soft and balmy, birds were tearing about the sky like rockets, courting and building nests, and the wall-flowers smelling sweet underneath the window.

"I've sent Auntie May a card," Mother would announce, "to ask if it's all right for us to go over on Saturday."

Back came a message to say "be sure and come in time for dinner". So we set off, our Mother, Betty, Mick, Ben and me. My two elder brothers, Bern and Bunt, were old enough to do a job of work on Saturdays and they did not think much of it when they knew that we were going off for the day. Ben and Mick rode in the pram while Betty and I trailed behind. Before we had gone far I started to cry—I wanted to have a ride too. In the end our Mother gave in, she shoved Mick up nearer Ben and then balanced me on the end of the pram. My weight almost tipped it up. It was not long before Mick started wailing "our Mollie's sitting on my legs, they be gone to sleep." Protesting strongly I was dumped down again.

"Catch hold of her hand, Bet," our Mother shouted, "and help her along. If there's going to be crying I shan't bring you next time," she threatened, so I wiped my eyes and nose on the sleeve of my coat and strode along as fast as I could. I certainly did not ever want to miss the treat that we knew awaited us at Auntie May's. You see, Uncle Patrick worked in a grocer's shop in the town a couple of miles away, and one of his perks was that he was able to buy odd bits of bacon, and for three pence he could get enough to make a big pudding. And always when we visited them Auntie May would make the loveliest boiled bacon and onion clanger that I have ever tasted. It slipped out of the wet pudding cloth onto a great oval dish, a big damp, shiny, steaming, succulent pudding. Then with her hand raised high in the air Auntie May would plunge the knife into it, revealing slivers of pink bacon and releasing a luscious smell which made our nostrils twitch and our mouths water.

"You certainly makes a good pudding," our Mother remarked, as we all tucked into the feast, "and just look at the bacon!"— indeed there was more bacon than onion.

"Well, it's nice to see you all enjoying it," Auntie May said, "our little Marion wun't touch it." White-faced Marion sat at the end of the table, toying with a boiled egg that she had insisted on having. But to us the meal was a feast of the gods.

Auntie May was comfortably rounded; she had wispy grey hair and a complexion like an orange, and false teeth that clicked and clacked as she spoke. Uncle Patrick was as lean as a greyhound in training, a quiet solitary man who liked nothing better than to work in the peace of his potting shed or sit in their stuffy front parlour and read. "Read hisself sill, thas what he'll do," Auntie May would cry, "dun't know how I ever come to marry such a mouse, that I dun't."

But we all knew. One hot summer, after the First World War, she had cornered him in her father's pigsty and seduced him. Every night young Auntie May, a slip of a girl of seventeen, lured young Patrick Day into the pigsty. For two whole weeks the passionate love affair lasted. He had never been known to even look at a girl before. "Didn't know what he'd got it for," Auntie May told her friends afterwards. At the end of the fortnight Patrick emerged, a wiser, sadder young man, and a few weeks after Auntie May's mother made arrangements for them to marry as quickly as possible, "to make an honest girl of our little May," she told the villagers. And twenty years on, history repeated itself. But instead of a pigsty it was an air-raid shelter at the bottom of their garden. There their only child Marion, blonde and as pretty as her mother had been, fell in love with an American soldier.

"Our poor innocent little Marion," Auntie May cried when she discovered that her daughter was pregnant. After the war Marion and her husband Jake went off to the U.S.A. where they helped to populate an already over-populated country, producing eight boys in as many years.

But during those uncertain years between the wars Auntie May and Uncle Patrick were very kind to us. We often walked over to see them or they came over to visit us. Whenever we called, Auntie May would produce a piece of home-made cake or a few sweets tucked away in an old tin. If we called on a Sunday then Uncle Patrick would be home and he would always find something interesting to show us. One year it would be a robin who had built her nest in his old gardening jacket as it hung behind the potting shed door. Another time a pair of blackbirds built their nest in his pea sticks that were propped up against the wall.

"Can't disturb 'um," he told us. "I shall have to go awf on my bike presently and cut some more sticks, thur's plenty down Ham Lane." And the blackbird sat there, bright-eyed and trusting, as Uncle Patrick showed us the beautifully made nest.

Another thing we enjoyed was playing with Marion's toys; she seemed to have so many, more than we ever dreamed of. But we were a bit too boisterous and rowdy for her really, and I got into awful trouble once for teaching her cheeky rhymes. Of course she had to go and say one in front of the vicar when he had called to see her father one day about the local fête. She went dancing into the room and swinging her knickers in her hand she chanted:

> What's the time?
> Half-past nine,
> Hang your knickers
> On the line,
> When the soldiers come along
> Hurry up and put them on.

At that time it seemed strange to us children that Auntie May and Uncle Patrick did not seem to be the least bit interested in one another, and only spoke to each other when it was absolutely necessary. Auntie May used to tell everybody that he'd "never touched her" since the pigsty affair; she would say, "reckon he's all dried up, 'tis a wonder I ent gone off with somebody else affor now."

Then one day, soon after Marion had sailed off to America for good, Uncle Pat was missing. He had set off on his bike for work as usual with no more than a flask of tea and his dinner tin in an imitation leather bag, and his old raincoat strapped on the carrier where he always carried it in case of rain. But he never arrived at the grocer's shop where he had boned bacon and skinned cheeses and patted butter into half-pound slabs for the last twenty-five years. Rivers were dragged and hospitals phoned but no trace of him could be found. And the village gossips reckoned that he had probably gone off because he could not stand the sight of Auntie May any more. Which was what *had* happened, but it was over two years before we really knew the details.

Poor Auntie May was furious when it finally dawned on her that Uncle Pat had just walked out on her, and after waiting over a year without a word from him she sold up their little home and went off to America to live with Marion and Jake and their children, only to die of a heart attack within three months of settling there.

Then about a year after her death a curious thing happened. Back came Uncle Patrick, now a changed man. There was a jaunty air about him and he had got the merriest twinkle in his eye. And he had brought with him a small gentle woman—the new Mrs Day in fact, and it was obvious that they worshipped each other. The villagers accepted them at once, and only then did we learn what had happened to him since he had ridden away on that lovely May morning over two years ago.

He told our Mother, "It was such a perfect morning, Kate, and I thought to myself as I rode along that life was too short and too precious to waste any longer, and I asked myself, what had I done? What had I seen in all those years? It wasn't until I got within a hundred yards of the International Stores that I made up me mind that I'd ride off, away from everything. So instead of gettin' awf me bike when I got to the shop, I just kept on going. I didn't really mean to hurt May, I should have told her I was going awf, but honest, I only made me mind up on the spur of the moment. Well, I rode and rode for miles, only stopping to have a bit of food and drink, then when evening come I was miles away and I thought, ah, Pat me boy, you can't go back now, so I slept agen an old hay-rick, must have slept like a babe too, for the next thing I knew was that a farm worker was prodding me and asking me what the hell I was doing. Well, we had a little chinwag, seemed an under-standing sort of chap and he said that his gaffer would most likely take me on, casual like. They were a bit short-handed and there was plenty of hoeing and beet singling to be done. By golly, Kitty, I don't think I've ever bin so tired before; them first days hoeing nearly creased me. I was that weary at night I went straight off to sleep. Ah, I had lodgings with the fellow who'd found me under the rick, nice couple they was, he and his wife, so I stayed with um all that summer.

"Then come autumn I moved on, I'd saved quite a bit of my earnings so felt that I could now see some of the countryside, before winter set in. Oh, I did enjoy that autumn; I rode through the Lake District, through the industrial north and on again through Yorkshire, where the sheep graze over the mountains. One day, in November, I was riding through a biggish town, so I stopped at a provision shop to stock up my supplies, always carried some food with me I did. Well, I went into the shop and talk about chaos. Apparently that morning the manager and two assistants had all gone down with 'flu, the undermanager had been taken off to the local infirmary after being involved in an accident, that only left two young girls in the rather big grocers. I asked for cheese, there was no one to skin one they said. I asked for bacon, there was none boned. Neither of the girls had been there long enough to learn either of these jobs, people were coming into the shop and going out again pretty quick when they found they couldn't get what they wanted.

"So I said to one of the girls, 'Could I help you, miss? I used to work in a shop like this. I could skin a cheese or bone a side of bacon for you.' The girl looked at me a bit hard, didn't know what to say, poor devil, she'd never been in charge before. And besides, I expect she thought I'd make off with the takings when her back was turned. So I said, 'It's all right my dear, you can keep your cash desk locked. I shouldn't blame you, you've never set eyes on me before.

"Well, three weeks later I was still there, ah and I got on well with the staff and customers. When the manager come back he offered me a permanent job, but I turned it down. 'Twas time I set out over the hills again. Well, I spent most of the winter in Scotland. Think of it, Kitty, I'd hardly been out of the village before. I done mostly farm work, there was plenty of threshing work and potato sorting on a big farm where they grew special seed spuds. As I come back down the country I called at a Post Office in Leeds where I'd written and asked our vicar to write to me. There were four letters from him, course they was months old, and in one he told me about May's sudden death.

"I felt quite sick for days, guilty conscious I suppose, walking out on her like that, but there hadn't been a shred of real love between us.

" 'Twas a beautiful spring that year, the countryside was so green and fresh and new and I thought that it was a sort of omen, maybe, it was a sign of a fresh start for me. Again I done all sorts of jobs, sometimes I even called back on farmers that I'd worked for the year before; they was all pleased to see me and would set me to work if there was any extra hands needed. Then I got a job near to Rotherham. I felt quite excited, but didn't know why, it was in this town that I'd worked in the grocer's shop. So I called to see how they all were and was given such a welcome. Then the girl who'd been scared for me to help them came into the shop. She'd been out to the storeroom, she blushed when she saw me, and that was that. We just fell in love there and then I reckon. Course I know I was eighteen years older than her, but it didn't matter. So I got a job in another shop in the same town and lodged with her folks. We never got married till just before I came back here. Somehow I wanted to come back home, course I didn't know how the people would be, me riding off like that, but I thinks most of them understood."

"Well, as the years went by Uncle Pat became a parish councillor and a church warden and both he and his wife took an active part in the life of the village. They died within a week of one another; she went first, then Uncle Patrick just slipped away having nothing left to live for. They are buried together in the little over-grown churchyard; a simple tombstone reads

> "Lucy and Patrick Day
> died June 1963
> Servants of God"

At Uncle Patrick's wish their ages were not carved on the stone for, as he told the vicar once, "In my eyes my Lucy is still a young girl and I'm her young man, the only pity is that we didn't meet years ago."

# 11

# Dumble Dads and Foster Mums

It was just a turn of fate that Clarrie Ford became our Auntie.
For Clarrie was already 'bespoke' to a young man in the next village
where she came from, when she met our Uncle Fred, and he, at
that particular time, already had an 'understanding' with eighteen-
year-old Daisy Simms, who lived next door to him and his widowed
mother. Daisy was away in service and Uncle Fred only saw her
about twice a year. But they were saving up to get married; Daisy
already had a fair-sized bottom drawer, filled with embroidered
cushion covers, crochet-edged tablecloths and beautifully made
chemises, knickers and camisoles, lace-edged and feather
stitched.

Fred was saving all he could; he had an old tea caddie, which he
kept for safety under the bed. The caddie was filled with florins
and half-crowns, along with several silver threepenny bits.

He was under-gardener up at the big house. There were four
gardeners employed there and his wages were eighteen shillings
a week, but it was a good steady job and there was a chance that
he might become head-gardener in time.

But one day in early summer, about two months after Clarrie
Ford had arrived at the big house, where she held the post as under
parlourmaid, a strange thing happened that was to alter the lives
of Clarrie Ford and our Uncle Fred Brown. Mind you, Fred had
noticed that there was a new maid who sat along with the other
servants when they attended evensong in the parish church, where
he also worshipped. From his pew at the back of the church he
noticed that the new maid wore a pretty mauve hat with a sprig

of flowers in the front; she was an attractive little thing, neat and perky. Not that she ever glanced in Fred's direction, but each Sunday after the service he would wait by the church gate, along with the other lads of the village to glance shyly at the group of servants as they came out looking very prim and precise, except the kitchen maid who was always at the back of the group; she was a hefty girl and used to turn round and poke out her tongue at the young men standing there awkward and uncomfortable in their best, tight-fitting, navy-blue Sunday suits.

But on this particularly lovely summer evening Clarrie somehow got parted from the little group of servants as they came out of church gate, so Fred quickly walked alongside her and started to chat, first about the weather, then he asked her about her job.

She started to tell him, then said, "Really, I should go along with the others, we are supposed to keep together."

"Well," Fred replied, "we'll just follow behind them," and for a little while they walked along together not speaking a word.

A few minutes later Fred said, "We could go the field way, it's a lovely walk along by the river, and just as quick as the road way, we shall be at the big house as soon as they," he said nodding in the direction of the little group walking in front.

Well, Clarrie said that it was a beautiful evening and she had never been along by the river path. As Fred helped her over the stile he noticed that she had dainty small feet and slim ankles. Whatever would Daisy think of him? Fred though, here he was, strolling along the field path on a lovely summer evening with a strange girl, and she was laughing up into his eyes quite friendly like.

Fred showed Clarrie a yellowhammer's nest tucked away in an old willow tree. He was glad that now she seemed in no hurry at all to rejoin the other girls.

Then Fred said, "Would you like to sit down for a few minutes?" It was pleasant and peaceful with the sun quite warm. He spread his handkerchief on the grass, for Clarrie to sit on, "Just so you won't get no grass marks on that nice suit," he added.

Clarrie sat down, carefully smothing her pale grey skirt so that only her trim ankles peeped underneath. Fred sat stiffly beside her, as she told him about her home back in a small village in Wiltshire.

Suddenly, Fred had the shock of his life.

Up leapt shy, timid Clarrie, screaming and shouting "Tak um off, take um off." She was dancing and jumping about on that sunny bank like someone demented.

For a moment Fred did not know what to do. He thought perhaps she was throwing a fit, like one of the boys in his class at school used to. Then she started to pull her skirt up—above her knees—still shouting take um off, take um off, over and over again. Then Fred noticed that her long white drawers and petticoat were covered with small brown objects; poor Clarrie had been sitting on a bumble bees' (dumble Dad's) nest and they were stinging her in the most delicate of places.

"You just hang on," Fred cried leaping to his feet, then he knelt down beside the poor girl but, short of taking her drawers off he did not know what to do. Then he said, "I know what, I'll squeeze um dead and you shake um out." And that was how Bill Bates the head-keeper found them, Fred on his knees finding and squeezing the bees that were inside Clarrie's drawers and Clarrie shaking them down on the ground.

But that was not how Bill Bates *saw* them. Here was young Fred Brown, a good, clean-living fellow, supposedly engaged to Daisy Simms, who was working away in service, gamboling about on the river bank with one of the servants from the big house, and she was letting Fred fondle her thighs and her with her skirt held waist high so that he could do it.

And it was no good them trying to make excuses—he had caught them red-handed and he would report the incident at once to the Master and Mistress.

What followed during the next week or so was almost unbelievable; nobody would listen when either of them tried to explain, least of all Lord and Lady Speak for whom they both worked. Her

Ladyship sent for the pair of them the next morning and insisted that they should get married as soon as possible. If this scandalous thing should get to the ear of their friends Lady Speak said they would be the laughing stock of the county.

"You'll make an honest woman of her young man," she went on, "not here in the village, oh no, we can't have that, I'll fix it up at Sodbury registry office for next week, the sooner this dreadful business dies down the better. You can have the small cottage at Penn Lodge," she went on, "I'll send Dawkins along to see that it's cleaned up, then we'll find some bits and pieces to furnish it until you can buy your own."

"B—but," stammered Fred, "I'm already sort of engaged to be mar . . . ," but her Ladyship cut in. "You should have thought of that last night young man; now off you go the pair of you and get on with your duties. Come and see me at eight o'clock tonight, and by then I shall have fixed up when you can be married. And thank your lucky stars young man that my husband didn't sack you on the spot, and you young woman can leave the day you marry, I don't want anyone fainting and falling about here."

Poor Clarrie and Fred; they had only known each other for a few hours and, here they were, destined to spend the rest of their life together.

Clarrie wore her best mauve costume to be married in and cook pinned a few flowers on it for her. Fred wore his best navy serge suit that he had had for his father's funeral five years previously. His widowed mother, just as bemused as the unfortunate pair, decided not to act as witness at the wedding.

"I'd not no Sunday go tu meeting clothes, Kitty," she told our Mother, "And I was worried tu death, I didn't know how I was going to manage without our Fred's bit of money and, anyhow, I was living in a tied cottage, and I knawed the squire ud ave me out, once our Fred was married."

But things turned out fine for them all. Fred and Clarrie were as happy as sandboys, with Fred's mother living with them Clarrie used to help in the fields whenever there was a bit of extra work to do; they had four strapping boys, although it was two years before the first was born.

We did not visit them often, although they only lived a couple of miles away. But if we could get the woman at the lodge gate to let us take a short cut through the park, then it was only about a mile. Each time she said the same thing, ' 'tis more than my life's worth, to let you through, if ever I was found out my Herbert 'ud get the sack.' But she always gave in, 'go on then, but keep to that little grass path and be quiet.' We thanked her and squittered quickly into the green tunnel of hazel bushes that led to Auntie Clarrie's and Uncle Fred's cottage.

It was ten years since the Dumble Dad incident; Fred's mother had died and Clarrie no longer helped on the farm, but stayed home and looked after their four growing boys and Uncle Fred.

Auntie Clarrie was in a bit of a state the day we called. Her broody hen that had been sitting on thirteen lovely brown eggs had suddenly "gone off her brood", and had left the eggs, which Auntie Clarrie said were already pipped and should have hatched out the next day.

"I've been all over the place," she cried tearfully, "to try and borrow a 'sitty' hen, but you know how it is at this time of the year, everybody doing the same thing, trying to get a few chicks off so as they gets a good supply of eggs come next winter."

"Whatever shall I do?" she went on. "I can't set on um me-self, can I?, but if I don't soon do summut about it it'll be too late, they chicks ull be dead affor they be out of the shell."

"Ent you got a foster moster?" our Mother asked her.

Clarrie looked bewildered, "A what?" she cried.

"Well have you got a mop head? a new one would be best," our Mother said. Clarrie rushed out to the back kitchen and came back almost at once clutching a new mop head. "Bought it only last week," she said, "when I went into Witney market."

"I shall want a piece of thickish string," our Mother said, as she went down the garden path to where the big square box which

served as a hatching house was, as was customary, the open front
of the box had spars of wood fixed across, so that a broody hen
could just get her head and neck through to feed, and later the
chicks would be able to get through the slots to the run, but the
clucking mother hen would be inside. But there was no broody
hen in this box, just a nest of eggs carefully covered with a piece
of flannel to help them keep warm.

Our Mother quickly tied the string to the mop head, then
lowered it down onto the eggs, covering them with the woolly
strands. Then she got a piece of wood, tied the string to it and fixed
in on to the top of the box, adjusting it so that all the time the
mop head rested on the eggs.

"Now when the chicks begins to hatch out," our Mother told
her, "you just gently raise the mop head about a couple of inches,
that'll keep 'um warm enough and they'll never know the differ-
ence."

Auntie Clarrie was overjoyed. "God bless you, Auntie Kitty,"
she cried, "I shall never be able to thank you enough."

After they had had a cup of tea our Mother said we best be
getting off home, and anyway it looked like rain. So off we traipsed,
creeping stealthily along the grass path. We spoke in whispers
lest anyone should hear us, then slipped silently through the little
gate at the side of the lodge that the lady had left open for
us.

We turned our faces towards home, when suddenly the heavens
opened—it did not stop to rain, but came down like stair-rods.

We sheltered for a little while, but we were all drenched anyway, so our Mother said we might as well get off home. "Come
on," she cried "best foot forward," and we trudged along wet,
cold and miserable.

Suddenly, holding her left foot up Betty cried, "Look at my
sole." It had almost parted company with the rest of the
boot.

"God in Heaven, what shall I do?" our Mother wailed, "ten
shillings and sixpence I paid for them last week and the man said

they was leather, it's nothing but cardboard," she cried. "We shall have to tie it up with something." The loose sole looked like a big gaping mouth.

Up went her skirt and she wipped off one of her elastic garters which held up her stockings. Then she twisted it double over the arch of Betty's boot and around the sole. "Well, at least it won't get any worse," she said. "Your father will have to mend it before you wear um again."

With nothing to keep her bagging stocking up she just took it off and stuffed it in her coat pocket, "I'm Diddle didle dumpling," she said laughing at her misfortune, "only its one stocking off instead of a shoe."

A couple of days later Uncle Fred arrived unexpectedly, on the back of his bike, he had got a big brown parcel. He handed it to our Mother saying, "Clarrie hopes you won't be offended, Kitty, but her was that grateful for what you done, we got thirteen lovely strong chicks, ah, every one hatched off and they be doing fine. You see, Kitty," he went on, "always at this time of the year her Ladyship gives us a big box of clothes, her 'ave done it ever since our hurried wedding, but some of it ent no good to us and Clarrie thought as you could make use of it."

"You know what the good Book says," our Mother cried as she unfolded the parcel of clothes. "Cast your bread on the waters", she said, as tears of thankfulness trickled down her cheeks.

Although we were quite content to roam the fields and lanes near home, or play games near the cottage, when our Mother did suggest going out, even to the next village, we children would get very excited. We always enjoyed the jaunts we made with her. She made them so interesting that they seemed to be a cross between a nature study and a general knowledge lesson, and lots of fun all rolled into one. She would point out and explain things of interest to us and show us what we could or could not eat when it came to wild berries, fruits and fungus.

"See these," she cried one day, pointing out a 'death cap' mushroom with its greeny white cap, "*Never, ever* touch one of these or you know what you'll be doing, in very quick time too, pushing up daisy roots."

"And just look at this," she would say, pausing for a few minutes to show us bee orchids that we might otherwise have missed, or perhaps a clump of wild thyme, which would start her reciting Shakespeare:

> I know a bank whereon the wild thyme blows
> Where oxlips and the nodding violet grows
> Quite over-canopied with luscious woodbine
> With sweet musk-roses and with eglantine.

"Ah now, there was a clever man, Shakespeare," she said, "I've read quite a lot of his works, started when I was at school. The teacher would lend me books of her own, cos I'd read everything in the School Library betime I was eleven. I used to smuggle a bit of candle into my bedroom whenever I could, so that I could read in bed—course I wasn't supposed to and I'd half screen the lighted candle under the bedclothes if I heard my parents about. Course, reading was frowned on in them days, well by ordinary folk anyhow. But," she went on with a proud tone in her voice, "I've never forgotten what I read, or regretted it either."

A trip which we always enjoyed was one that we usually made about twice a year, to the little village of Peasfield, about three miles away and where an old friend of the family, Aunt Annie Edwards as we called her, lived. She had been a great friend of our Mother's for years and was particularly kind to her when our father died, and the friendship continued when our Mother married again, for Aunt Annie Edwards thought that our step-father was a grand fellow.

She lived on her own in a tiny stone cottage, low-beamed and with small lattice windows whose sills were always crammed with scented geraniums.

"Go on," she said to me one day, "just pinch a leaf between your finger and thumb and sniff." I did as she said and put my hand to my nose savouring that haunting lingering perfume, a smell which to this day still brings back a clear picture of Aunt

Annie Edwards and her little stone cottage, with its garden jam-packed with flowers, a colourful crowded patch which she did all herself.

On one of our visits our Mother happened to remark how strong and healthy the plants and flowers in the garden all looked. Aunt Annie admitted that she "emptied the slops" over her roses, and she went on, "You must agree, Kitty, they be fine blooms, and the day as they fits we up with water closets u'll be a sad day for we, 'cos the only manure as I ever uses is from my old privvy—well apart from the horse droppings I gets from the road. Oh ah," she went on laughingly, "thurs a proper fight between I and my neighbour as to who gyets out with a bucket and shovel first. Bless 'e, I be out there that quick sometimes a-gatherin' it up, that's still steaming when I puts it on the gyarden."

Bless her heart, she need not have worried about the coming of the water closets for it was the late 1960s before her village was put on the sewer and by that time Aunt Annie had been dead for twenty years.

One of the reasons for our visit to Aunt Annie's in later summer was that, across the fields from her cottage, were the remains of an old orchard where trees bearing small blue early plums, which we called cunigars, grew. These small plums made the most delicious jam—although our step-father declared that it was "all stones".

"Ah," our Mother would reply, "them as eats most jam, gets the most stones, and anyway if I was to take um out when I made the jam thur'd be nothing left, so you'll have to put up with um."

Of course we girls, Betty, Mick and I, loved to get plenty of stones, so that we could play "this year, next year, sometime, never" with them, in a vain attempt to find out when, or if, we should get married.

We would wait for a postcard from Aunt Annie telling us that the plums were ripe. Our Mother usually received the card about the last week in August. When we grew up we would go over on our bikes, but while we were young our Mother either pushed the smaller ones in the pram or in Kitty Moore's bath chair, with us older ones tagging on behind.

One hot humid August day our Mother looked at the cloudy sky. We had planned to go to Aunt Annie's straight after our dinner, a make-do meal of bubble-and-squeak and cold bread pudding.

"I don't reckon that it'll rain before night," she said, as we all went out to view the weather prospects. "Ah," she cried excitedly, pointing to a break in the clouds, "that'll be fine all right; as long as you can see a bit of blue sky up thur big enough to patch 'Billy Peglar's britches', that rain will keep off." This was one of the old weather predictions that her father had passed on to her. He had been a shepherd all his life and was very knowledgeable when it came to weather lore.

As we trudged along the roads we saw several farm wagons as they passed to and from the harvest fields. They were pulled by great sweating cart horses, and the carts were so wide and the country roads so narrow that we had to squeeze ourselves up against the hedge as the big Oxfordshire waggons went by. They were simply overflowing with sheaves of corn, and the hedges were draped with corn stalks where the brambles had caught them.

"Come on," our Mother shouted to us, "you leaze all you can, whatever we gets will feed our hens. Not like when I was young." she went on, "then we had to go leazing properly, not for the hens but for us. When we had got a nice lot my dad would take the corn up to old Jack Wheeler the miller and he'd grind it into lovely white flour. Ah," she went on, "that flour used to last us all winter fer cakes and puddings and my mother used to make her own bread in the winter if the roads was too bad fer baker Clegg to come our way delivering."

The time passed quickly as our Mother told us tales of her youth, so that the journey to Peasfield seemed to take no time at all.

We arrived at Aunt Annie's about two o'clock. She had got the kettle singing away on the hob and soon we were all enjoying a hot cup of tea and a chunk of her dripping cake. Presently she said, "Who'd like another piece?" Five pairs of hungry eyes faced Aunt Annie as we replied in a chorus, "I would, please." It had been a long, hot walk and we were always hungry.

As soon as the teapot had been drained of every drop and our Mother and Aunt Annie had had a good chatter, we made our way up the bumpy cart track, each armed with bags and baskets, and with Aunt Annie striding out as if she was off on a five-mile walk, her walking stick helping her along. But the stick was really for hooking down the high branches. There was always a risk that someone had been to cunigars before us; usually we were lucky, although I remember two or three times when we found very few plums. Then Aunt Annie would make it up to us by stacking the well of the old pram with pots of her home-made jam, and may-be a jar or two of honey, which she took from her own skip that she kept at the end of her long garden. And a bottle of her rhubarb wine for our step-father.

Sometimes we would walk up the fields beyond the old orchard to gather early blackberries, especially on one occasion when we found no plums at all; Betty had gone on in front and we could see her busily picking blackberries. Then she came running back towards us, she was eager to show our Mother what a lot she had found, when suddenly she caught her foot in a bramble and she, and the almost full basket of blackberries, went flying onto the thick grass.

"Oh, dear," our Mother cried as she sank down on to her knees, "we shall have to pick up as many as we can as they're too precious to waste." Suddenly she grabbed at something in the grass and shouted excitedly to us "Look what I found!" In her hand she held a struggling leveret, that had been so frightened by the noise of humans that it had crouched petrified in the grass hoping that no one would see it. Quick as a flash our Mother held it up by the back legs and whacked the kicking animal on the back of its neck with the side of her other hand and in a moment the once vibrant body was still.

"Ah, that will make us a good meal," she said as she knelt down again to retrieve the rest of the spilt fruit, then again there were wild shouts of joy, "If the Lord don't come he sends," she shouted, using one of her favourite expressions, and she held out her careworn hands which were full of large, pink mushrooms. She called to Aunt Annie so that she might share her good fortune and they knelt down on the grass together almost as if in prayer. I can see my Mum now kneeling there, her straw hat askew, her face russet red with excitement. I heard her say to Aunt Annie, "If our Bet hadn't tripped with them blackberries we shouldn't have had neither leveret nor mushrooms, ent we the luckiest people."

" 'Tis funny," Aunt Annie remarked, "I've lived yer all me life and I've never knowd mushrooms grow in this field affore; still," she went on, "now I comes to think of it, old Jack Phipps did have his horses up yer fer a time, back end of last summer I thinks t'was, and they do say as you'll find mushrooms wherever horses have been."

Content with our finds we wandered back to the cottage. Then another cup of tea and another slice of Aunt Annie's dripping cake and we were off on the road towards home again. We turned to wave to her before we passed round the bend of the road and out of sight of her little stone cottage. She stood there waving to us, a tall, well-built upright woman despite her sixty-odd years.

I must have been about seventeen when I last visited Aunt Annie, but by then she was "too ett up wi rheumatism" to make the journey up the rough cart track to the cunigars. I was wearing a pair of my eldest brother's trousers (I had borrowed them unbeknown to him), and Aunt Annie was disgusted. "Making yourself look like a fellow" she said, "I don't know what the world's coming to."

But my brother found that I had worn his only good pair of flannels, for they were covered in green where I had brushed against the old tree trunks as I gathered the plums; and to make

Mollie's first visit to the seaside

Aged sixteen, on her sister's new bicycle

(*left*) Ben, the author's brother, playing cricket in the Moors, a rough field opposite the family cottage in Ducklington. (*right*) Betty, the author's sister, aged sixteen

Dick Clarke, a cripple who lived in Ducklington, with brother Joe (the village postman), his wife and a young relative

matters worse I had got oil on the turn-ups off my old bike chain, which I had carefully oiled to make the bike ride easier.

My brothers and step-brothers continued to go to cunigars each year up until the outbreak of the Second World War, but by then I had found other paths to tread.

## 12

# Rhymes and Relations

Thinking back, I am sure that our Mother was the inventor of occupational therapy.

When we got too big for hidings, or when she realized that they ceased to have the right effect on us, she thought up jobs for us to do that were far more effective than a good clout behind the ear. Sometimes she found us jobs to do just so that we would not get bored and consequently into mischief, and sometimes because she did not want us to play with the children who happened to be out in the street, and sometimes just out of plain cussedness.

One day Mick and I had to take the two youngest, Ben and Denis, for a walk: our instructions were to keep them out of our Mother's way until dinner-time, a matter of about three hours.

"And take them up the Curbridge Road," she called to us as we pushed the old pram out of the gate.

All went well for the first hour, then the boys began to get restless, so we stopped by one of Strange's fields. I lifted them out of the pram and we all went into the field and sat down by an old pond. When we got tired of throwing stones in the boys started chasing each other round it, while Mick and I gathered up some kindling wood. I had just turned round to put the wood in the pram when there was a yell from Denis who had fallen into the green, slimy pond and was floundering about in the middle. I waded in and dragged him out: he had swallowed some of the stinking water and was coughing and spluttering and very wet.

"We'd best get him home quick," I yelled. Denis was very prone to chesty colds. If we left him to dry it would be tempting providence. So we packed the boys into the pram and started to push like mad, running and careering down the road as if we were being chased by the old nick himself. But we had forgotten about the great potholes, we hit one at speed and over went the pram, boys, wood and us. Ben and Denis began to yell at the tops of their voices. Ben had a nasty cut over his left eye and was bleeding like a stuck pig. Denis, thankfully, had landed on the wood, which had saved him from hitting the rough road, and seemed none the worse for the fall. We picked up the wood, piled it back in the pram, carefully sitting the boys on top and crept slowly home.

Our Mother was furious, "You'll go without your dinner, both of you," she cried as she bathed Ben's cut eye, "you shan't go out any more today, you can spend the rest of your time ravelling."

Mick and I looked at the sack in the corner of the room, it was full to the brim with bits of cloth, mostly of the looser woven type. All this had to be unravelled. First we had to cut the cloth into smallish squares, then each thread could be pulled out in short strands. Our Mother used it to fill cushions and pillows, and sometimes she would even add some to an old mattress to help make it a little more comfortable. Ravelling was a long, boring job and one that often fell to Mick and me. To make the time pass quicker we would tell each other rhymes and jingles, laughing and giggling into the piles of unwoven threads. Even so, if she thought that we were enjoying the job, our Mother would shout, "And shut up that gigglin' or I'll knock your two heads together." As soon as she was out of earshot we would start again.

"You heard this 'un?" Mick asked. "Teddy Simpson told it me yesterday, it's a good 'un."

> In days of old
> When knights were bold
> And paper wasn't invented,
> They used blades of grass
> To wipe their ass
> And went away contented.

We nearly exploded as we tried to stifle our laughter, getting redder and redder in the face as we did so.

Suddenly I wanted to go to the lavatory. I shot off down to the bottom of the garden. The day was hot and sultry and I had to shoo dozens of wasps and flies out of the privy before I could sit down and do "me bounden duty" as Missus-next-door called it. There was a good supply of torn-up newspapers and magazines hung up behind the door. This was another of our Mother's occupational jobs. If you were a bit cheeky to her she would soon have you tearing paper into sizeable squares, then you had to pierce a hole through each piece with an old steel meat skewer and thread the lot into a piece of string and hang it up behind the door—for the use of.

It made good reading material too. You could pull off a couple of sheets and sit there in comfort then, just as you got to an interesting piece, there would be a hurried search through the thick pad hoping to find the rest of the story. I reckon I did most of my reading down there. Living in a crowded cottage as we did, the lavatory was the one place where you could find a bit of peace—apart from the flies. But even if there wasn't much to read, it was nice to sit there with the door open at about forty-five degrees, with one foot on either side of the door, one to keep it open and one to stop it from shutting. Then if you heard somebody coming down the path, all you did was to move your left foot out of the way, give a quick shove with your right one and the door would shut.

But, undisturbed, you could sit down there for ages with the sunshine pouring in, relaxed, comfortable and dreaming. Or maybe watch a spider catch and eat a fly that he had caught in the huge cobweb which always seemed to fill the far corner, or count the leaves of a piece of waywind (bindweed) that had forced its way through the wooden sides of the lavatory and was winding its way up to the low ceiling, or just sit there and sing, as Missus-next-door did sometimes. There was only a wooden partition between our privy and theirs, so you could hear everything that was going on. Once when Bern, the eldest, was in ours and Missus-next-door was in theirs, she started to sing in a high piping voice, "I be fer ever Blowing Bubbles" and my cheeky brother called out, "Ah and that ent the only thing you be blowing, Missus."

When she told our Mother that Bern had been cheeky to her, he had to either go and dig the garden all day or spend the whole of Saturday and Sunday wooding, as a punishment.

Suddenly the quiet air was shattered, our Mother in full voice hollered from the house, "Come on out of there, Mollie, you've been down there half an hour already. If there's anything wrong with you, you can have an extra dose of senna pods tonight." At that threat I dragged my knickers up quickly and was soon back indoors, back to the eternal ravelling.

Dinner time came and went, but our Mother kept her word and we remained in the corner, our fingers automatically pulling out threads, our eyes and minds on other things. About half-past three she said, "All right, I think you've been punished enough, here, take this," she said handing us each a huge chunk of bread and treacle, "and go on out to play for an hour." We grabbed the food and were out of the gate as fast as our legs would carry us.

"Wur yu bin all day?" Sally Parker said. "We've had some lovely fun, you should a bin here."

"Well, we are here now," I said, "what shall us play at?'

"Let's go and see if Perrit's plums be ripe, shall us, they be gone walking up to Witney, so they wunt be home yet."

We ran off down to the village. "Come on, let's go the back way," I cried. So we made our way down Coltham which would bring us right at the bottom of Perrit's garden.

The plums hung fat, ripe and pregnant, luscious red and gold in the quiet orchard. They were Mrs Perrit's pride and joy. She always won first prize at the annual flower show with her bottled Victorias and her lovely red plum jam.

A few wasps and blue bottles buzzed about on the tops of the trees, sampling the over-ripe fruit: the afternoon was hot still and motionless, the plums waiting to be picked.

Pounds and pounds of those super summer fruits we ate. From tree to tree we moved, selecting only the biggest and best.

"Crickey," Sally Parker said, "I couldn't eat another, not if you was to give me a pound note. I be that blowed out I could bust," she cried sprawling herself out on the warm grass. We flung ourselves down beside her, shutting our eyes, listening to the soft buzz of the wasps and flies, we were as full up and contented as a sty full of newly fed pigs.

Suddenly I heard Mr Perrit's affected voice saying, "I think there's someone in the orchard, dear, I'll just change my clothes and go down and see."

Of course Mr Perrit tried to be what we called "a bit on the posh side", and would not have dreamed of going down the orchard in his best suit, not if all hell was let loose, which was very fortunate for us, because as soon as he and his wife had disappeared into the house we crept out the back way and were paddling in the nearby Windrush when he finally walked down the orchard. He stared across at us, a bunch of squealing girls splashing about in the sunshine, then he shook his head and went back indoors.

A few days later, when we got home from school, Mrs Perrit and our Mother were chattering by the gate. Mrs Perrit was just saying, "Are you sure it wasn't your Micky and Mollie? My hubby said they were down that way."

"I'm sure it wasn't my children," our Mother replied sternly. "I kept them in most of the day because they'd tipped the boys out of the pram in the morning, so they spent the rest of Saturday ravelling. No. I'm sure you're mistaken, Mrs Perrit, and before you start accusing my children, you just get your facts right," and she flounced off indoors her face red with temper.

"Now we're for it," I whispered to Mick. "She will ask us if we was down there and we shall have to tell the truth."

A loud yell from the house sent us scurrying indoors—"Damn and set fire to it," our Mother cried lifting a smoking saucepan off the fire. "Drat the woman and her blummen plums, I hope somebody pinches the rest of 'um, she made me forget me pudding and the darn thing has boiled dry." The pudding was quickly transferred to another water-filled saucepan.

"Go on, Mollie," she said, handing me the burnt black pot, "see if you can get that clean and hurry, I shall want it to cook the spuds in soon." So I was despatched to the back kitchen and scrubbed away with salt and elbow grease for what seemed ages before I could get the thing clean; by then our Mother had thankfully forgotten to ask us if we knew anything about Mrs Perrit's vanishing plums. What retribution would have followed had she found out that we were the guilty party did not bear thinking about at the time. But now, when I sample the delight of Victoria plums, I am magically transferred back to the tidy orchard in Ducklington, to the fat, ripe, forbidden fruit, the juice of long-forgotten summers, of hot fly-filled afternoons, and the cool evening peace of the Windrush.

Some of the jobs our Mother gave us to do were not always because we had been disobedient, but just so that we would learn to use our own initiative.

When we were quite small she would make us rag dolls, but as we got older we were encouraged to make our own. Giving Mick and I a pair of her old stockinet knickers, she said, "Go on, see who can be first to make and dress a doll." We slit the knickers in half, taking a leg each sewing it up and stuffing it with ravelling to resemble the body and head of a doll. Of course we did not use the whole piece of material. I suppose the finished doll was about sixteen inches long. While our Mother had always used a bit of black wool for doll's hair, we wanted something different, so we walked up to Witney and prowled about round the railway goods yard looking for thick string that had been thrown on the ground. When we had gathered enough we took it home, unplaited the coarse yellow string which made lovely blond, crinkly hair. Shoe buttons were used for eyes and nose and a bit of red wool embroidered the mouth. The clothes were also made of wool which we gleaned from around the seats in the Leys, a recreation park in

Witney. It was to here on summer afternoons that the ladies from the town pushed their prams; while their babies were taking advantage of the fresh air and sunshine, their mothers chatted and knitted. Quite long pieces of wool, from casting off and on and unpicking mistakes were thrown down. Match sticks were used as knitting needles, for small fingers match stick knitting was ideal. The whole operation of making and dressing a doll took a matter of weeks, for much of our spare time was taken up with looking after the younger boys, doing errands and helping in the house.

But through the hidings and the jobs came something else. Our Mother was really preparing us for the future: she knew what she wanted for her children and went all out to see that everyone of us had a good chance of getting it. She certainly was not 'soft' with us as were many of the village mothers with their children. At the time we hated this strict attitude of hers, but it was for our own good in the long run.

Much to her disgust, our step-father used to come home and tell us ditties or parodies that he had picked up at work. There was not really anything wrong in them, but it was just that our Mother did not encourage us in that sort of thing. Still, he used to argue with her and say that if he did not tell us them we should most likely pick them up from the other children.

"That," she said to our step-father, "is taking the Lord's name in vain," when he was singing a ditty to get young Ben to take a Beecham pill. These pills were not too bad if you swallowed them quickly, before the sweet powdery coating was sucked away, but after that they were quite bitter. And this pill that Ben had so far refused had lost all its sweet covering. Despite her grumbling our step-father sang again:

> Hark the herald angels sing
> Beecham pills are a very good thing
> Easy to take and meek and mild,
> Two for a man and one for a child.

As young Ben opened his mouth to laugh, our step-father popped the pill in, and it had gone down before Ben realized it.

One day I was in the back kitchen singing away as I washed up when, wham, I had a good cuff behind the ear.

"What was that for?" I asked our Mother, as I rubbed my stinging ear.

"That," she said, "was for singing that dirty song, and don't you ever let me hear you singing it again, or you'll get a clout the other side." I was dumbfounded. All the kids were singing it, we had sung it at the top of our voices as we came home from school—

> There was a bonny Scotsman
> At the battle of Waterloo,
> The wind blew up his petticoat
> And showed his 'ow-du-do'.
> His 'ow-du-do' was dirty,
> He showed it to the Queen,
> And she gave him sixpence
> To keep it nice and clean.

Another time our step-father was walking down from the garden unconsciously singing a parady to 'Sonny Boy'. Mother was in the wash-house and just as he passed he sang:

> I know what you're after
> That place above my garter.

"What did I hear you sing?" she yelled rushing out of the wash-house and facing him. He did not answer, but she went on, "I don't care what you sing at work, but don't bring your filth home. What if the children heard you?"

But she need not have worried, we had already heard it but were much too young and green to know what he was singing about.

Sometimes relations and friends would drop in unexpectedly to see us, often round about teatime, and most likely we would have nothing but a cup of tea to offer them. On these occasions, while they sipped tea and chattered to the rest of the family, our

Mother would disappear into the back kitchen for a few minutes. Quick as a flash she would mix together flour, marg, sugar, a handful of mixed dried fruit, and an egg and spread it on to a sandwich tin and slip it in the oven of the valor oil stove which our step-father bought her. Then she would come back into the room and ask sweetly if anyone wanted another cup of tea, and by the time the kettle had boiled again and the tea cups refilled, the visitors were thoroughly enjoying the hot, crumbly cake, which our Mother called "rub up".

Life was like that, you simply lived from one day to the next, for nobody could afford to keep much of a store cupboard. Even things like cake and jam were eaten almost as soon as they were made. But our parents fed us well, food came first and foremost in our house.

Almost every morning we had porridge for breakfast. Our Mother made it that thick you could have stood a flagpole up in it. But the skill came when she produced tasty stews and soups from next to nothing. Rabbits were always plentiful and we ate them often. The funny thing was, it seemed, that I was the one that nearly always got the head, which had very little meat on. If I protested about the lack of meat, the family would say, "Go on—there's the brains, you eat 'um, you can do with them, they'll do you good." So I would pick away at the head; there was a *tiny* bit of meat on the jaw-line, and of course the white soft brains, which, at the time, I really believed did me good.

One night we were all sat round the table, having just finished our meal, and Bunt remarked laughingly, "The Lord be praised, the belly's raised!" and we all started tittering.

"What did I hear you say?" our Mother cried angrily.

And Bunt only about twelve at the time, repeated the rhyme, only to be rewarded with a good cuff behind the ear—for taking the Lord's name in vain. "Where on earth did you hear that?" our Mother asked him, she was furious.

"One of the boys at school said it after he'd had his dinner," Bunt explained.

"Well, don't you let me hear you say it again," she cried. "You know how quick these others pick things up. And less of that tittering," she yelled to the rest of us, "or you will get a good smack."

At that moment I let out a loud cry, one of my baby teeth had come out. It has been loose for days, waggling about every time I had eaten anything. We scrambled down from the table, all eager to see the tooth burn.

"Burn, burn blue tooth, Please God send me a new tooth," I said solemnly, flinging the tooth on to the fire, as I did so. Immediately a small blue flame sprang up from where I had thrown it.

"Ah," our Mother remarked, "it burnt quick and clear and bright, that means that your new tooth will come through soon and it will be firm and strong."

This little ritual of throwing teeth on the fire was always carried out when any of us youngsters happened to lose one.

There were lots of funny little beliefs and sayings in those days —for instance, if you sneezed we used to say that it meant you would be kissed, cursed, cussed or shake hands with a fool. When this happened in our house our Mother would immediately thrust out her hand, so that the sneezer might shake it. Not that she was anybody's fool, but it saved you being cussed or cursed, and at that time we were a bit too young for kissing to have any effect.

And if your nose itched, then you were going either to—

> Run a mile
> Jump a stile, or
> Eat a pancake in a field.

Itching or burning ears meant that someone was talking about you, and the saying was that it was

> Right your mother
> Left your lover.

And itching hands were significant too:

> Scratch them on wood
> Sure to come good

was one belief, another was if your right hand itched you would receive some money, but if your left itched then you would be paying some out.

But if the bottom of your feet itched, it meant that you were going to walk on strange ground. If your new boots or shoes squeaked when you first wore them, folks said that this was a sign that they had not been paid for, and children would tease each other unmercifully about this. I know I got a good hiding from our Mother one day, after I had suggested, quite seriously, to respectable Mr Hills, that he could not have paid for his, because his were squeaking like mad when I walked home with him from Witney.

And bad luck would surely befall you if you forgot to put a coin in the pocket of a coat or suit, when it was first new.

And there were peculiar country cures which people often practised. An old gypsy woman told our Mother once that the best thing to cure a baby's sore bottom or ease spreeze on children's legs was ashes from elm wood. Simply burn some elm wood, let the ash get cold and then rub the affected parts with it. She also told her that bleeding could be stopped by laying a thick black cobweb across the wound, but I do not think she ever tried that one.

# 13

## Summer Days, Summer Ways

We loved the hot sunny days of summer, the long hot, dusty days when we played almost all the time. Winter with its severe frost and snow was completely forgotten, and never it seemed had it ever rained, always it had been hot, sunny and dusty.

Our stone-built cottage was cool enough, but outside the heat hit you like a frying pan. So we spent most of our time by the river. In the mornings our Mother would load us up with a big bag of bread and jam, and a bottle of lemonade made with a ha-porth of yellow sherbet powder to last us all day.

The shaded lane which led to Gooseham was waist high with nettles and purple vetch and grass, except for a narrow path that we had made where we constantly trailed along it. The lane led out to Wilsdon's field and to our beloved river Windrush. One summer the field was almost bare of grass, for the long, hot spell had lasted several weeks, and huge cracks had appeared in the ground and one of Wilsdon's cows had caught her hoof in one and as the poor animal had tried to free itself it had broken the trapped leg and the cow had to be destroyed, but at least the meat was good and it was later sold in one of the butcher's shops in the town.

The field was covered in cow-dung, cow clats as we called them, and they were sun-baked as hard as concrete and were thick with yellow horse-flies which stung us and fetched our skin up in big red weals. But even the cow clats had their uses, some of the villagers collected them up in this hard, solid state and put them on the copper fire where they burnt like wood, but let off a terrible smell as the smoke from the fire floated over the village in the still summer air.

And so the long hot summer wore on. Some of the wells in the village almost dried up, ours got very low, so low that, as we let the bucket down it scraped the bottom, disturbing the gravel and making the water cloudy. Mrs Wheeler's well was completely dry, even the ferns growing on the sides were parched brown. We leaned over gazing into its cavernous depths watching the newts darting and climbing about, desperate for dampness.

The drought meant hard work for villagers. All the housewives saved the water from the weekly wash for watering the gardens in an effort to save the withering crops, or to slosh down dirt paths to help lay the dust. "When it do rain," our Mother threatened, "I shall rush out and stand in it with no clothes on, that's the only way I shall ever cool down," but of course she never did.

Throughout the summer she was at constant battle with fleas, daily searching the hems of sheets and blankets for them, cracking them dead with her thumb nails when she did find one. It was not that we were flea-ridden like two or three of the families were, but when you played and fought or sat next to children who were, catching them was inevitable, one hop and jump and the little beggars would soon settle on a nice bit of fresh flesh. Our Mother only had to see a tell-tale bite on us and then nothing rested until she had tracked the offending flea down and firmly cracked and killed it.

Flies were a menace too. The only deterrent at that time was a tuppenny flypaper. This was quite an ingenious thing, a long, brown, sticky, treacly thing about two feet long. But when you bought it, it was cleverly rolled up inside a very small carton. You pulled the sticky strip out by a tiny loop whereby you hung the flypaper up, with the little carton that had held it still firmly stuck on the bottom end. Most people hung their flypapers up in he centre of the room, usually over the table where the flies seemed to congregate. They just flew on to the sticky strip, stuck to it and died. But I could never make out whether it was simply because they could not get away or whether there was, in fact, some poison on the flypaper. We were so plagued with flies in the summer time that a fresh paper only needed to be hung up for a short while before it was simply black with dying insects.

One day, bored with the long, hot, dusty day, we decided to play soldiers with our cousins and a newish boy to the village called George Wilkins. George was very popular with the children because he had a German helmet that his father had brought back from the war. We all fought George because he was the enemy, but we could not hurt him, at least not his head, because of the wonderful helmet. On this day George was shouting to us, "Go on, you buggers, hit me, hit me", and we all set on to him thrashing him over the head with sticks. Suddenly George keeled over; he was as white as a sheet, his eyes were rolling, he was frothing at the mouth, and his arms and legs were making jerking movements. We were so frightened, we just looked at each other and then tore home as fast as our legs would carry us, daring anyone to breathe a word of what had happened. Later on we discovered that poor George was subject to fits, and our hitting him about the head had nothing to do with him passing out and foaming at the mouth. All the same he never asked us to play soldiers with him again, or whack him over the head.

Another morning during that summer our Mother announced that Mick and I were not to go out to play until we had each picked a cockerel. These were two that we were going to have for Sunday dinner. "We might as well eat them as keep them for Christmas," our Mother cried. "They will eat me out of house and home, darned hungry things." So she caught a couple of them and, holding them in her strong, brown hands, she stretched their necks and killed them, and handed one each to Mick and I to pick the feathers off. Then she left us to get on with it, the hot bodies, lifeless now, lay on our laps—they picked better warm our Mother reckoned. We pulled away at a few feathers, loath to work on this hot, sultry day. The little hen fleas began to creep up our arms annoying us, it was far too hot to do any more we decided.

"I know," I said, "let's hang um up in the hen run and let the other hens peck the feathers off for us." Mick agreed that it was a good idea. So we tied the cockerels up by the legs and hung them up and sat back and waited for the fowls to do the work for us. It was hot and smelly sitting there in the muck-covered hen run but we did not mind, at least we were not doing anything. I fetched out a grubby piece of paper and a stub of pencil from my frock pocket and started to write my very first poem.

> Once I had a rabbit
> All of my very own
> And its little wooden hutch
> Was lodged upon a stone.

I decided there and then that I was going to write poetry and that when I left school I should not go to work but stay at home and write wonderful poetry. Goodness knows how long Mick and I sat there mumchancing as the hot afternoon wore on.

Suddenly our Mother's face appeared round the side of the chicken run. "I thought you was too darned quiet to be up to any good," she hollered, her face red with annoyance. "Get on and pick those birds, or I'll thrash you till you can't stand." Of course we knew that she would not be as hard as that on us, but the threat of a hiding had us both picking feathers off those birds a darned sight quicker than we had ever done before. When we eventually crept out of the hen run our Mother was waiting for us; she just clipped our ears and sent us off down Gooseham to see if the boys, Ben and Denis, were all right.

We rushed off, thankfully escaping the threatened hiding. Down by the Windrush we paddled along with the rest of the village children. Mick and I swilled our faces, necks and arms to rid ourselves of the hen fleas. They do not live on humans, but they do irritate you while they are crawling about on you. Some of the bigger boys climbed up into the willow trees which stood like a row of drunken sailors along the river bank. Then the lads leapt

The author's three brothers:
(*right*): Bunt, outside the family
cottage, Wayside. (*below left*):
Ben, aged about twenty-two.
(*below right*): youngest brother
Denis, taken during the Second
World War

The author, aged about twenty, on holiday in Madeira. She had saved up for three years to make this trip

out of their perches into the river, splashing us all over so that we
might as well have been swimming in our frocks we were that wet;
but we soon dried in the warm sunshine.

Our strip of the river Windrush was mostly shallow and gravelly,
a beautiful winding river. In some parts, the lovely green water
weeds grew: they moved silently, floating and waving in that
gentle stream, looking for all the world like the tresses of water
maidens. Minnows darted around your feet and tickled your ankles
if you stood still, but the crayfish kept well out of our noisy way
only coming out at night when all was quiet and still.

Just a few yards downstream from where we swam, Wilsdon's
cows would stand hock high in the Windrush, cooling themselves
and drinking, their great pink tongues picking up the water, with
the sun catching the droplets as they fell, turning them into rain-
bow colours so that they looked for all the world like jewels tumb-
ling from a treasure chest.

There were a few deep pools along our stretch of the Windrush,
like Parson's hole and Holland's hole where some of the grown-ups
bathed. And running almost parallel with our river, but further
away from Ducklington, was another stream called Cogg's brook,
a much deeper and swifter flowing river. And it was in that river,
somewhere between Ducklington and Witney, that a group of
young men from the town bathed naked almost every Sunday
during the summer-time. Everybody knew that it went on, but it
certainly did not bother us, nobody sneaked about to look or anything; anyhow we had seen boys bathing naked before and our
young green minds did not know that grown-ups looked any
different. But we knew that we were not supposed to go anywhere near and we did not. It was one of those things that were
taken for granted. They were just a bunch of very respectable
fellows, Oxford bagged and very with-it: shopkeepers' sons and
bank clerks mostly, who enjoyed this perfectly innocent weekly
jaunt and swim.

But one summer just before I left school I struck up a friendship, of which my Mother greatly disapproved, with a very pretty

I

girl. Rosie Brown her name was and she was quite a bit older than I, about eighteen, I think she was. All the villagers said that she was fast and flighty, but I thought that she was marvellous and longed to grow up as pretty and popular with the boys as she was. Wherever we went the village lads used to follow, but Rosie would have no truck with them. "Blummin' lot of hobble-de-hoys," she said. "I wouldn't go to the bottom of our stairs to meet any of um."

Normally our Mother never interfered with our friendships, she left it to us to make our own judgement about people, but in this case she did try very hard to put me off going out with Rosie Brown, saying that she would lead me astray, but I could see no wrong in her. Then one day after a fierce argument about my friendship with Rosie, our Mother dared me ever to go out with her again.

I cried and sulked, but it did no good.

"If I so much as hear that you have spoken to her," our Mother bellowed at me, "I shall keep you in every weekend until you have learnt your lesson. You are not to have any more to do with her and that's that."

But one hot summer Sunday afternoon I was mooning about over the meadows near our cottage when I met up with Rosie again and, forgetting my Mother's threat about keeping me in at the weekends, I readily agreed to show her a short cut over the fields to Coggs brook, where she said she particularly wanted to go.

We trudged over the grassy meadows, it was hot and close and Rosie seemed to be in such a hurry.

Suddenly we rounded a bend in the river and she cried joyfully, "Ah, there they are."

And just a few yards away, frolicking about in the summer sunshine were several young men, laughing and splashing about in the river—then I realized who they were.

"We 'ent supposed to go anywhere near them," I cried, "our Mother ses if you do they'll chase you naked," and I started to back away.

"Don't be such a silly," Rosie said. "They would be frit tu death tu come out of that water in front of us," and she walked boldly along the bank and stood on the grass in front of the bathers scanning their faces. Seeing the one she was looking for she called out.

"Johnny, I've come to see you."

"Go back," the young man called in a very cultured voice, "go back and I'll see you in the town tomorrow lunchtime."

"I want to see you today, now," she pleaded with him. "I'll shut my eyes while you get out and dress if that's what's worrying you." But the young man refused to move.

She came back to where I was standing.

"I'll get that bugger out you see if I don't," she whispered to me. "Just because he got his friends with him he don't want me, well, we'll see," and she marched up to the neat piles of clothes, each topped with a clean folded towel, that the young men had placed on the grass.

One by one she picked up the heaps of clothes. "Whose is this?" she called out and one by one the young men answered her and shouted to her to put them down. There was only one pile of clothes left. With a cunning look in her eye she gathered them up in her arms and began to walk very slowly across the field, away from me and the bewildered watchers in the river.

"You best get off home," one of the men called to me. "This is no place for you." I stood where I was for a few minutes thinking Rosie might not like it if I went back without her.

Suddenly the young man who she had spoken to swam to the river's edge and rose out of the water. He looked like one of the Greek gods whose statues I had seen in a museum at Oxford.

Then he ran across the field after Rosie. She turned round and saw him coming, so she too started to run, then she tripped over a tussock of grass and went flying headlong into the field; at that moment the young man caught up with her and flung himself down beside her. I turned and ran for home.

A little while later I heard that the young man, a bank clerk, had married Rosie and that he had been transferred to another part of the county. And that I thought was that. But a couple of years later Rosie came home bringing a most beautiful child with her. The marriage had not worked out, the young man's parents thought that he had married beneath himself and never accepted Rosie and some time later they were divorced, a shocking thing in those days.

I became quite friendly with her again, she was not really as bad as folks made out. Her earlier behaviour was just a desperate attempt to get away from home. Then she told me what had happened to her before she and her father and stepmother came to live near our village.

"You see," she told me, "my mother died when I was ten and my father, desperate for someone to look after me, advertised for a housekeeper. Well, this person Eva came along and before you could wink they got married. They did not tell me until afterwards and I was that upset. You see I loved my mother; we three, my dad, her and me was as happy as sandboys, and whereas my mother was very kind and loving, this Eva was as hard as nails and bossed us about something awful. I think that she was jealous of me and the fact that my Dad was fond of me. But she soon put a stop to that. They had a terrible row with my stepmother threatening to leave. After that there was no kind words or playful teasing from my Dad, only an indifference that I, as a child, could not understand. Oh, she fed me all right, but that was about all. Then, one day, coming up to my thirteenth birthday it was, quite suddenly she became nice and friendly towards me. She had a lovely silver watch, a round one about as big as half-a-crown it was. She wore it on a fine chain which hung round her neck. The watch had delicate engraving on the back of it and I thought that it was beautiful.

"Then she said, 'Tell you what young Rosie, you shall have it for your birthday.'

"Well—I was that excited I didn't know what to do and I couldn't understand why she should want to part with it, and I eagerly awaited my birthday, but just two days before she said that the watch was missing and she wanted me to swear that I had seen old Jake, a man who worked on the same farm as my father, and who sometimes popped in for a chatter, take the watch. She had walked into the town that afternoon and notified the police, and when they came I was to say that the old man had taken it. Of course I told my father as soon as I had the chance. There was a terrible row between him and my stepmother, then my father got on his bike and rode into the town and told the police that what she had said was a pack of lies. She thought that was the end of it but the next day the police came and gave her a good telling off. It appeared that she was a gambler and she used to bet on horses and had, in fact, pawned the watch. Apparently this was a put up job, her pretending she was going to give it to me and then say someone had pinched it. You see the bookie was worrying her for the money she owed him, so she had to find it from somewhere.

"Then a few weeks after that one of the fellows who worked on the farm attacked me as I was coming from school. Course I didn't really understand what he was doing, but I knew it was not right. He had a knife and I was frightened to death. Three times he 'made love to me' as he called it before he let me go.

" 'Don't you dare tell nobody,' he said, 'or I'll slit yer throat with this,' he said waving his knife. I rushed home crying and hysterical, my clothes were all torn and I was covered in blood, I was in a terrible state.

"Then the police came and the doctor and then they took Jimmy away and locked him up and I think he died some years later still in the asylum where they put him. Well, the doctor said that he didn't think that I would be pregnant after such an attack, but my stepmother wasn't taking any chances, and for weeks after she had me jumping off five-bar gates, leaping from hayricks, and then she dosed me up with gin and vinegar and nutmeg, all these were old wives' tales of how to get rid of a baby. And all the while she kept saying that if I had a child nobody would employ me when I left school and that everybody would look down on me for the rest of my life. I can tell you that she made my life hell, and all this at thirteen years old. Still, thankfully, I didn't have a child.

"But from then on all I wanted to do was get away from home, I didn't care how it happened as long as I was not under the same roof as my stepmother. Anyhow you know the rest of the story.

"Then last year my stepmother went off with the postman, so I'm back home looking after me Dad and of course young John-boy."

Then the war came along and I lost touch with Rosie, but I heard that in about 1944 she married a Canadian pilot and after the war went back to his home in Montreal.

I wonder if she ever thinks of those far-off days, of lush green meadows, flower-filled and speckled with butterflies, a river bank lined with drunken willows and the happy laughter of youth drifting over the cool clear water of Coggs brook.

# 14

# Winter

While the summers of my youth seemed always to be hot and blazing, the winters in their turn were mostly very cold, at least so it always seemed.

"I reckon this cold weather comes from the Russian steppes," old Mrs Adams remarked one day, her nose glowing multi-coloured in the frosty air.

And when someone asked Dan Dore if he was sweating, when the temperature was well below zero, his reply was, "The only place I sweats is at the nose end." And that was probably something that we all did.

We would set off for school wrapped up warm in almost everything that we had. "Go on," our Mother would say, "run all the way and then you will be hot as toast when you gets there," and we would all tear off at a rare pace, slapping our thighs and whinnying and snorting, shouting "giddy up" to ourselves and rearing and galloping about like a lot of young colts, and our faces red and glowing when we arrived at school. On these occasions we stayed at school for dinner. We each had four thick slices of bread and dripping and a screw of newspaper containing a spoonful of cocoa and sugar. Miss Spencer, our headmistress, would put a kettle of water on the top of the huge tortoise stove, so that we could make a hot drink at dinner time—no milk, just cocoa, sugar and water. But to us, on those cold days, it was like nectar of the gods.

The classroom was as cold as charity, except for the immediate area by the fat, round stove, which was situated behind the teacher's table. My desk was very near to the door and when the wind was in one direction it used to whistle round my legs, causing me to have chilblains, at least that was what our Mother said caused them, for no other member of the family had red, swollen legs like mine. And every night, when the warmth from the fire made the chilblains itch I nearly scratched my legs raw. But, before I went to bed our Mother would cut a big, raw onion in half and give it to me to rub on my inflamed legs. Really all the onion juice seemed to do was cool them down, but at least it brought a bit of comfort for a while.

Mind you, one of the old wives' tales to cure chilblains was to immerse your feet in a full chamber-pot and bathe the chilblains. This I did—anything for relief—but again I think it only cooled my throbbing legs. Then there was the fact that I had to endure the indignity of bathing my legs in somebody else's pee. I must have stunk to high heaven during the wintertime, what with the smell of goose-grease and camphorated oil on my chest and onions and pee on my feet and legs.

That particular old wives' tale was also supposed to cure bald heads too, but I never heard of anyone trying it; if they did and it had not worked I do not suppose that they would have admitted defeat or the indignity. But the cold, hard spell of weather continued for several weeks.

Our step-father met old Billy Tanner walking down the road one day muffled up in an old army coat and thick scarf.

"Cold enough for you, Billy?" our step-father called.

"Ah that 'tis, Ben," the old fellow replied. " 'Tis that cold in my cottage I goes tu bed with all me clothes on and then I byent warm, and do you know?" he went on, "you mightn't believe what I be going tu tell you, but that bin so cold in my bedroom this last few nights that have froze the piddle in the jerrypot." And he shuffled off his boots encased in a pair of old socks to stop him from slipping on the frozen ground.

Two years before this particular cold spell our two-holer vault lavatory had been replaced by a bucket lavatory, and while the old one only needed to be emptied twice a year, the bucket, with seven children and two grown-ups using it, had to be emptied daily. As soon as our step-father came home from work he knew what his first job was. He would come into the yard, prop his bike up by the wash-house, go in and get his spade, and proceed down the garden collecting the full bucket on his way, and take the contents up to the end of the garden and bury it.

But during the extremely cold weather this became a bit of a problem. The ground was frozen solid. He tried digging a hole with a pick but it was impossible; so for a while the offending contents were strewn over the top end of the garden. By the time the weather got warmer some of the material had broken down but the paper was still there, blowing about in the garden, so we were sent to gather it up and make a bonfire of it.

Still, while the cold weather lasted we fed the birds and slid nightly on the frosty pond or on the flood-frozen meadows opposite our house.

At this time Bern, the eldest, had just left school and for about a year worked for a farmer Mr Parker of Barley Park Farm. One of his jobs during this particularly cold winter, was to help clear some woodland, so along with another young fellow, whose nickname was Skeecher, they hacked away with billhooks and hedge-slashers keeping themselves reasonably warm, and cutting and clearing away all the scrub, small trees and bushes. The big trees, of course, were left to the tree fellers to cut down. The lads had to work methodically, clearing up as they went along. First all the brushy sticks were set on one side, these had to be tied up in neat bundles of faggots. Later on these would be sold to local bakers, who used them to heat their ovens. Some cottagers bought them too, to chop up for fire lighting. Pea sticks and runner bean sticks would also be cut and tied up and these too would be sold in the village or in the nearby town. All the rubbishy stuff like blackberry bushes, twigs and gorse had to be burnt, and all day long the lads would keep a huge bonfire going, always remembering of course to work with the wind in their faces and the bon-

fire behind them, so that they did not have the smoke blowing
into their faces all day. With no other means of providing themselves with a hot drink, the lads would heat water from a nearby
pond (sometimes ice) in an old tin that they found in the hedge,
setting the tin in the red embers at the bottom of the bonfire.
"We 'as it just like tramps do," Bern said, "two spoonsful of tea
and a bit of sugar, and we drinks it straight out of the tin and
that goes down a treat."

But that wood was a godsend to our parents—it saved them the
expense of buying coal.

All her life our Mother was very friendly with a Mrs Bowles who
lived further down the village. She was a widow woman, a Lon-
doner with three daughters and a son. Betty was pally with the
girls because they were round about her age, and they all used to
go dancing together at the Corn Exchange in Witney on Saturday
nights. And the Bowles family, like us, had a wind-up gramophone,
so one Sunday night we would all walk down to their house and
take a few of our records and the next week they would all come
up to our house with a few of theirs.

They were lovely, unforgettable evenings, with lovely, unforgettable songs. We would all of us join in the singing, accompany-
ing John McCormack as he sang in his rich, deep voice Macushla,
Macushla, or Layton and Johnstone as they dreamily serenaded
us with "I'll bring a Love Song", "My Blue Heaven", "Have a
Little Faith in Me", "Shalimar", "Souvenirs", and "Goodnight
Sweetheart", or the songs that a local man Moss Turner recorded,
for a big record company—"With a Song in My Heart" and "A
Little Kiss Each Morning, a Little Kiss Each Night", lovely lilting
melodies that still bring back memories of the happiness we found
on those Sunday evenings. Of course with our one track minds
we just had to spoil some of those songs, like "The Sheik
of Araby", which we insisted in adding "without a shirt"
after almost every line which made the song both funny and
vulgar.

Most likely we would finish off the evening with nothing more than a welcome cup of cocoa, made with water and just topped up with milk, before we left for home. Then all the way back, and indeed all the next week we would be singing or whistling those songs.

One Sunday night we were walking back home having a good sing-song. As we rounded Collis's corner to the strains of "Ramona", we met old Luke Atkins. He was wandering from one side of the road to the other. Luke was a beer-swigging, baccy-smelling old devil who was often the worse for drink.

"Lovely singing," Luke called out in a slurred voice, "but why don't you sing 'Just Like the Ivy I'll Cling to You?"

"Ah," our step-father replied laughingly, "I reckons you'll want summut to cling to or else you will never get home in your state." So we left old Luke there propped up against the wall while we made our way home on that clear, frosty night carolling "Just Like the Ivy" especially for old Luke.

Then the temperature began to get a little warmer, and we woke up one morning to find the countryside covered in a deep heavy fall of snow. Every tree and branch and plant was covered in the powdery stuff as if a giant had come overnight and spilled caster sugar over the whole village. Snow was worse than frost as far as we and our boots were concerned. When it was frosty at least it was dry and so were our feet, but the wet, soft snow soon pene-trated our boots, saturating our socks and stockings. We only possessed one pair at a time, so it was off with them as soon as we got indoors. Our Mother showed us how to stuff our boots with newspaper, which absorbed the damp and padded them out so they did not dry hard and wrinkled. So in the winter evenings the old fire hearth was filled with drying boots.

Wellingtons were coming into fashion, but we could not afford any. But I remember how excited we all were when Betty, who at the time was working at the laundry in the town, came home with a pair of Russian boots which were absolutely the height of fashion, leather they were and knee length.

When we were not sliding on the pond or visiting Bowles's we spent the rest of the evenings by the fireside. I remember once Mick passed away a whole winter by making a doll's cot from out of an old shoe box. She made a minute mattress and a pillow, sheets and blankets, then draped the lid so that it looked like a super baby's cot, only to realize at the end of the winter that she had grown out of dolls and dolls' cots, and that she was almost old enough to go to work.

And sometimes, during the winter evenings, if he had not got a pair of our boots to patch up, or a puncture to mend, or his bike to repair, our step-father would amuse us for ages by making shadow pictures on the wall with his hands. He was very clever at this, manœuvring his fingers so that the animals and things that he made became quite realistic, because in the flickering candle or firelight they looked as if they were moving. He also made the appropriate animal noises, and we were fascinated by his interpretations of foxes, rabbits, ducks, cats and fighting cocks. To end with he always did a man chasing a ball across the living-room wall, the man had a long thin neck, and he made him disappear saying that he had gone to catch the animals up.

"That's it," he would say, "time you all went off to roost," so we younger ones would go off to bed. The bedrooms seemed freezing cold, but we quickly got warm once we were in bed and cuddled up to each other. Our Mother would come up and throw a thick coat over our feet for extra warmth and we were soon fast asleep.

Some nights we children would pass the time away by swopping rhymes and jingles. Where they all originated from I do not know, but we seemed to pick them up a lot quicker than we did lessons, remembering and recalling them much easier than we did dates of famous battles and crowning of kings and queens—especially if they were a bit rude.

> One fine day in the middle of the night
> Two dead men got up to fight
> I went downstairs to let them in
> They knocked me on the head with a rolling pin

The rolling pin was made of brass
They turned me up and slapped my ass.

But another version went like this—

> Not last night but the night before
> Two tom cats came knocking at my door
> I went downstairs to let them in
> They hit me on the head with a rolling pin
> The rolling pin was made of brass
> They turned me up and slapped my—
> Ask no questions
> Hear no lies
> Here comes a blackyman
> Playing with his—
> Higher up the mountain
> Greener grows the grass
> I saw a nanny goat
> Sliding on his—
> Cock your leg over the rope lady
> I'm selling three balls for a penny
> Just as long as there's any
> Hit the monkey on the belly
> And you'll win a box of cigars

And so you could go on, linking each rhyme cunningly so that you really didn't say the rude words. Betty told us this one that she picked up in service, it was what a cheeky kitchen-maid actually said to her very bossy employer:

> Yes Ma'am, no Ma'am
> Ma'am if you please
> Shall I stuff the duck's ass
> With the shells or the peas?

And the girl was packed off at a minute's notice for saying that.

And with the coming of the motorcar this little jingle was often recited:

> There was a little man
> And his name was Henry Ford
> He took a little bit of metal
> And a little piece of board

He took a drop of petrol
And an old tin can
And put it all together
And the darned thing ran.

Church singing was not left out either—we really had no respect for this harvest hymn:

All is safely gathered in
Docks and thistles tied with string
Some was thick and some was thin
But all was safely gathered in.

And instead of singing "Safe in the arms of Jesus" we bawled out:

Safe in the arms of a policeman
Safe locked in Oxford jail
Fourteen days hard labour
For pulling a donkey's tail.

Conundrums we were very fond of and sometimes we had the whole family guessing on really the most simple ones:

Stow on the Wold
Where the wind blows cold
And the cooks can't cook their dinner
Take Stow from the Wold
And Wold from the cold
And spell me *that* in four letters.

Or this one that we would write in friends' autograph books:

YYUR
YYUB
ICUR
YY4 Me.

Then quite suddenly the cold weather was over and the rains of February came with the banks of the Windrush flooding our low-lying meadows. I came across these doggerel lines the other day, they were scribbled on the flyleaf of an old parish magazine. I think they must have been written by a local person, but I have never heard them before:

> The floods were out at Ducklington
> One cold November day
> And all the ducks of Ducklington
> Were lost or gone astray.

If these lines were penned in the days of my youth I doubt whether the ducks had gone far, probably on to the flood water in the fields over the road from the pond. Here they would most likely find a different diet from the one the pond provided, fresh, succulent worms, water snails and beetles. But if the poem was written since the last war then the words are correct, the ducks have "got lost or gone astray".

For alas, there are no ducks now at Ducklington, and half the time there is no water in the pond either. I understand that some time ago it was cleared out, and cleaned so well that the Oxfordshire clay which lined it has all disappeared, and the only time there is water in it is when it has rained hard, and this soon soaks away. What a pity: that pond in our young days gave us so much pleasure, sliding in winter, playing mud pies in summer, and sometimes we were fortunate enough to find a duck's egg on the grassy bank. If we took it back to Mrs Collis she would reward us with a super piece of home-made fruit cake.

# 15

# The Green Years

When I look back to our growing-up years I realize that we were often very uncouth and cheeky. But it certainly was not for the want of trying, on our parents' part, to endeavour to make good citizens out of us. Both our Mother and step-father worked hard and long, striving all the while to bring us up properly, so that when the time came for us to leave school and start work, we might stand a fair chance with the rest of the world.

And because of this, the memories of many things that happened during those green growing-up years come flooding back—how proud of us our Mother was when we excelled ourselves in the school concerts—when I, out of all the school, won the Bishop's prize, and when Bunt had a drawing of an angel pinned up in the classroom for all to see, a very unusual thing in those days. His class had been learning the poem *Abou Ben Adhem* by Leigh Hunt:

> Abou Ben Adhem (may his tribe increase)
> Awoke one night from a deep dream of peace,
> And saw within the moonlight of his room
> Making it rich, and like a lily in bloom
> An angel, writing in a book of gold

and Bunt had drawn and crayoned a most beautiful angel, complete with golden pen and golden book, although someone was quick to point out that the pen the angel was writing with was in his left hand. "Anyhow," our Mother said, consoling him, "never mind, my boy, for all we knows half the angels in heaven might be left-handed."

And almost always she encouraged us to take part in the yearly concerts. In fact, without bragging, I can safely say that the members of our family were nearly always picked to take the star parts in the school plays, with somebody or other finding a bit of bright cloth for our princely robes. Then one year, when I was about eleven, I was chosen to be one of a group of four fairies and we were expected to find our own clothes. White plimsols and white cotton frocks and pale stockings.

"No," our Mother said firmly, "you are not going to be a fairy and that's that."

I cried, I sulked, and pleaded, but nothing would budge her from her decision.

On the night of the concert when parents were clapping and cheering the efforts of their children, I was perfectly miserable— worse too when the fairies came on the scene.

A few years ago I was shown some old photographs taken at these school concerts that we took part in. Amongst them was one of three fairies—the girls' faces were sweetly pretty, but the clothes, the black stockings, and one girl was wearing boots! I told our Mother about the photo.

"Yes," she replied, "perhaps now you can understand why I wouldn't let you be a fairy. I certainly did not want everybody in the village know that I couldn't supply your clothes and shoes."

But I did not see it like that. To me, it would have been no worse than me having to wear boots to school right up to the time I left at fourteen years old, especially as the other girls of my age were wearing shoes.

Is it just a middle-aged delusion, remembering the sun-drenched fields, when the long, hot summers timelessly slipped by, when grasshoppers leapt like kangaroos amongst the lush green grass and the yellow-hammers sang all day. Sometimes the mornings were unbelievably beautiful, with hazy mist hanging over the water meadows. Looking over the moors from our house you could see the herons leaping in the air from the stream, stretching their long wings in lazy flight, and the larks spiralling up out of the

K

grass, flying almost out of sight, just a tiny speck in a blue summer sky, and yet we could still hear their sweet singing clearly on the ground below.

We spent so many happy hours playing by, and in, our lovely river Windrush. Our favourite bathing place was Gooseham. But further downstream, beyond the flour mill was a quiet place we called The Ham. Here the river came through winding meadows, with the willow and hawthorn trees festooned with wild roses, almost dipping into the cool, rushy stream and the dappled sunlight shining on the water. No wonder we were as happy as bees in a buttercup, wandering along the river bank during those long, hot summer days.

We would often see the farm workers busy in the fields, hay carting and harvesting, dust covered, sunbronzed men they were with hairy chests like blackberry bushes, working tirelessly from sun up till sun down.

One day we came across Fred Franklin. He was lying under an "azzie" bush dead drunk, an empty yellow stone jar lay on its side. I picked it up and sniffed—coo, elderberry I should think it was. We left him there sleeping an innocent as a new-born babe. But I'll bet there was ructions when the farmer realized that Fred had not been working all that afternoon. But Fred was also a good gardener and quite a character, and people would often seek his advice about gardening matters, like Mrs Truscot who was having trouble with her marrows one year. "I can't get they flowers to set at no price," she told Fred one day.

"Ah," he replied, "you wants to 'noculate um with a hen's feather, that'll do the trick, you mark my words."

Another of his bits of advice was "When the elm leaves be as big as a mouse's ear, thas the time to plant yer kidney beans." Although our Mother said that Gloucester folk reckoned to plant theirs Stow Fair day which falls on or very near 12th May.

Old Fred had things to say about parsley too, when Mrs Salter complained to him that the seed she had planted had failed to come up.

"Ah," Fred said, "you got out of patience I expect and went and dug it up. That takes eight weeks fer parsley sid to germinate. You see," he went on, "that thur sid has to go down to the devil three times affor that 'ull ever start to grow, you just has tu give it time, that'll come through all right, but you go tu be patient. And another thing," he said, "don't you never transplant parsley neither. Thas one a the worst things you can do, it'll bring you nothing but bad luck and thas a fact."

"Do you know," Fred went on, "we nevers reckons to buy no vegetables, I can grow all we wants. Mind you, in the wintertime my Missus 'er 'ull go awf and get some a they 'urricane beans, cos 'er likes 'um with a bit of oxtail stew, and I can't grow they."

The hedge round Fred's cottage garden was always neat and tidy. But one year he was cutting it off almost to the ground. "That's a bit drastic, isn't it, Fred?" our Mother called to him as he slashed away.

"Ah, missus," he replied, "come spring that hedge 'ull begin to stoul out, and he'll be as thick as thick by next summer."

"Ah," he went on, "we don't half want some rain, don't we? I was telling the old parson the other day how dry it was, so he ses to me—

" 'Well Mr Franklin, I had no idea it was that serious, I will offer up a prayer on Sunday, maybe that will do a bit of good.'

"So I ses to him, 'Well sir, begging your pardon, but as long as the wind's wur tis, you'll be wasting yer time.' "

Fred gave our Mother a wonderful recipe for elderberry syrup. Excellent if you have a bad cold.

6 lb ripe elderberries
1½ lb sugar
Strip the berries from the stalks, put into a pan along with the sugar and simmer until the mixture is clear. Strain and bottle the contents. For a cold just put two tablespoons of the syrup in hot water and drink at bedtime.

To most of the villagers, our Mother must have seemed a bit unorthodox, to say the least. When other housewives were busy with their weekly washing or ironing, she would be taking us off on some jaunt or another. It only needed the sun to shine for her to make up her mind that she would take us out. "If that was to pour down with rain tomorrow, and I hadn't took you out today, it would be a day of sunshine that could never ever be brought back and we should have wasted it. I think the dear Lord sends the nice weather for us all to enjoy. Well," she said laughingly, "that's my story and I'm sticking to it."

On our way down the village we would have to pass Mrs Topson's cottage and Mrs Bolton's. These ladies were both very house-proud, their one aim in life was to be a better housewife than the other. It was a proper fight on a Monday morning to see which of them got their washing out on the line first.

Giving our Mother a disapproving look, Mrs Topson remarked: "Mornin' Missus, I'd a thought that you'd bin too busy a-doin' your ironing today, seein' as 'ow you managed to get your washing done yesday, to be traipsin' off with they children.

But our Mother did not keep to the ritual of washing on a Monday, ironing on a Tuesday, bedrooms cleaning on a Wednesday, and so on through the week, as most of the village women did. She did hers when the spirit moved her. One of her favourite expressions she used when she went out and shut the door on the housework was that she had "put a bit of salt on it, that'll keep it all right until tomorrow."

Mrs Topson was busy hanging the clothes that she had ironed out on the washing line to air in the lovely sunshine.

"Ah," our Mother said to her, knowing that it would rile the old lady, "most of mine gets ass ironed—I just folds it up and smoothes it out, then I lays it on the chair seat and puts a cushion on the top and everybody that sits on it, helps to press it."

"That wouldn't do for my Herbert," Mrs Topson replied, folding her arms and pulling herself up in a shrugging position. "Oh no, that wouldn't do for him at all," she repeated, her mouth set in a thin, hard line.

"Ah well," Mother replied sweetly, "it's just as well I 'ent married to him then isn't it?" And she walked off with us towards the woods.

Mind you, there was some of our washing that did not even get ass ironed. In fact, when the weather was hot and sunny and the washing dried in no time at all, our Mother did not bother to fetch hers in before it got "arched up", and really too dry for ironing. She would leave the sheets and pillow slips on the line until she was ready to make the beds—most likely late afternoon, then she would take them straight off the line and put them on the beds. If you have never slept in sheets that have been sun dried all day, *and not ironed*, then you have not lived. The delicious smell and the roughness of them is never-to-be-forgotten. The wonderment of drifting off to sleep at such a moment is heaven itself.

We called on elderly Mrs Carr, she had not been too well for a few weeks. "Just popped in to say how are you, we can't stop," our Mother called through the open door. Mrs Carr was a widow woman and quite poor, although she always kept two or three cats and made a drop of what she called (tonsil polish) home-made wine.

"Come in and set yerself down for a minute or two," the old lady said to our Mother, she was glad to see someone to have a little chatter to. "I wants you to try a drop of me last year's dandelion," she went on, "that ent a bad drop of tonsil polish, although I ses it meself."

She had her very own way of producing the most excellent wines. She told us how she went about making her dandelion. "I boils me flower heads up then when they be done I squeezes 'um between two saucepan lids, cos they be hot yu' see. Then I mixes the liquid with the sugar and a drop of lemon and orange juice, and when that's cooled down a bit I makes a slice of toast and spreads the yeast on it and just floats it on the top, and leaves it all to work for about a fortnight, affor I strains it off into bottles and corks it down. Course, if that haven't quite finished working they corks blows out, oh it's like being at the battle of Waterloo some nights, that it is."

We children had a drink of water and then went outside in the yard to play with the cats while the women chatted. One cat was called Lionel, farty Lionel, because of his bad habits, and the other a piebald looking thing was called Albert, although both of them were females. Mrs Carr used to say that her two cats had produced more kittens than she had had suet puddings. "As fast as they 'as 'um I drowns 'um," she told us one day. "I can't afford to keep no more than two or three cats at a time, so drowning 'ums the only way out. And they be useless as far as catching mice goes, I only keeps 'um for a bit of company."

"I'll let you into a secret," she announced one day, lifting up the red plush tassel-edged table cloth. "Look, this is where I keeps me wine while it's a-working." Standing on the floor underneath the table was her big red earthenware wine pan, it had a thick cloth over it. She lifted it up and showed us the contents. It was filled with fermenting mangold wine. "Thas my own patent mouse trap too," the old lady went on, "I caught two more of they little beggars this morning. Ah they mice 'ull do that wine a power of good. You see they gets in to me wine pan arter that soggy toast and then they slips in and drowns, and that wine 'ull feed on 'um, that 'ull be a drop of good wine, you see if that ent."

And although we children pulled faces at such a thing and pretended to heave at the old lady's tale, even we knew that wine fed on meat, because it was common knowledge that old farmer Kite, who made gallons and gallons of cider for his workmen, always reckoned to throw a sheep's innards into the brew, for it to work on. And his cider was not to be sneezed at either, 'twas some darned good stuff by all accounts.

And when our step-father, who worked at a brewery, used to help the brewer, he used to tell us a similar story. This brewery used to brew the beer in huge round vats which held hundreds of gallons of boiling beer. Our step-father used to have to skim the

froth or barm off it before it cooled ready for bottling. And because there was always a lot of grain about the place, it was over-
run with rats so they kept several cats to help keep the rats down.
Now the rim of this huge vat was about a foot wide and the rats
used to get on it to sample the barm. The cats then used to try
and chase the rats off, running round and round on the rim until
the rats more often than not made a dive into the beer and the
cats went straight in after them.

Our step-father would come home and say, "Do you know I ent
seen old Blackie," one of the cats, "for three or four days, but I
reckons I knows where he is." Then about a week later he would
say, "I've found what's left of old Blackie, his skin come up on the
brew today. You mark my words," he went on, "when I see my old
mates in the pub next week they'll say, 'My word Ben, thas a
drop of good beer this week' and I shall smile and agree with 'um,
but I shan't tell 'um why."

When I look back I marvel at the perseverance and energy
coupled with a brightness of spirit which our Mother possessed.
Even though, all through our growing-up years, she was dogged
by acute hard-upness. Despite this, she seemed able to sail through
life in a disordered, happy-go-lucky way.

She was always trying to make our cottage look bright and
cheerful, and one day you might arrive home to find every curtain
and cushion cover dyed rose pink, or even bright orange. She had
great faith in Drummer dyes; with a couple of these she would
transform the house whole, dyeing everything that she could lay
her hands on.

And one year she bought an out-of-date paper pattern book
from Margate's paint and paper shop in Witney. The book con-
tained about a hundred patterns of wallpaper, all different of
course, each measuring about two feet by one. Some of the paper
was cheap and cheerful, while others were glossy and of much
better quality, and she only paid sixpence for the book.

The very next day our step-father came home with a lovely
big stout wooden box, with a lid. It was so big that he had to walk

home from work with the box perched precariously on the saddle of his bicycle.

Our Mother swooped on it like a bird after a worm. "I can make a beautiful ottoman out of that," she cried, ignoring whatever use he might have had for it.

The box, which had held glass was quite well made, and he said that he had given a man a shilling for it.

Choosing the prettiest floral patterns from the old wallpaper book, our Mother set about pasting them, first on the outside of the box. Blue and pink trellis and roses covered one side, with the true lovers' knots and forget-me-nots graced the other, with Chinese lanterns and willow pattern on the lid. The inside she papered with damask white ceiling paper. Then she got our step-father to fix two hinges on the lid, on to which she tacked a big feather cushion. This provided us with an extra seat and also made a good storeplace for clothes.

We had it for ages. It stood in the recess under the window of the cottage. Of course through the years many different types of wallpaper graced its sides, but none of them seemed quite so beautiful as those odd pieces that our Mother first pasted on.

After the ottoman was completed she papered the larder with some of the odd paper. Normally this was simply whitewashed each spring, but the patchwork effect which we had that year was quite a change.

Even the lavatory got a new look. Instead of gazing at bare boards when you sat down there to do your "bounden duty" we beheld bright blue kingfishers diving into green pools, surrounded by bunches of purple and green roses arranged in eastern vases.

One of our neighbours, Mrs Pye, did not approve of such things —"getting beyond yerself", she remarked when she learned that our Mother had papered the lavatory. Still, there were several things about our family Mrs Pye did not approve of.

One day our Mother was hanging out the washing, which ran parallel with Missus next door's washing line. While our Mother hung Betty's fashionable french knickers on our line, Mrs Pye was hanging what we called her "free traders". These were the old-fashioned, white calico knickers, two legs on a band, tight at the waist and knee, but with a rather peculiar slit all up the back and front.

"Oh," Mrs Pye remarked with disgust, "I don't know what the world's coming to, that I don't, it 'ent decent, that it 'ent," she cried. "I should have thought you'd a put your foot down and not allowed your Betty to wear such disgusting things as them" she said, pointing to the pale pink knickers. "I wouldn't let our Flossie wear 'um," she went on, "cos I reckons that's tempting providence, that I do."

"I've never seen anything more disgusting than those you wear," our Mother replied angrily, "these my daughter wears are not half as bad. At least there's a bit of material where it matters, in the crutch, and that's more than can be said of your 'ever readies' because that's just what they are *ever ready*." And she walked down the garden path, her head held high.

Mrs Pye's stays were a bit old-fashioned too. Each week she would wash a pair of them, stiff, foreboding, whale-boned, armour-plated things that were greyish white, with laces up the back.

"I must have two pairs on the go all the while," she told our Mother one day, "one pair on, and one on the line. I 'ent like you, you know," she would remark, eyeing our Mother enviously, "you can take your corselets off and wash up and go about without 'um 'til they be dry, not me, I should catch me death of cold, that I should."

The thing was our Mother could not afford to have two pairs on the go, but at least she was not as badly off as old Mr Lines who lived down the village. His wife said that she used to wash his thick vest and long pants on a Sunday, and that he had to stay in bed until they were dry, so that he could wear them to work on the Monday.

Poor Mrs Pye, she was unfortunate really. She had, to use her own expression, "a bladder no bigger than a walnut" and was for ever shooting off down to the bottom of the garden to the lavatory. I remember Mick and I got a good cuff round the ears when our Mother caught us, singing at the tops of our voices we were, as the old lady went by:

> Have you seen me daughter sir?
> She can't hold her water sir,
> Every time she laughs, sir, she pees.

"I really don't know where you kids picks up these things," our Mother cried, "I'm ashamed of you, I am." And when she said that, we knew that she really was.

Only the day before she had heard young Ben singing a parody to a popular song, which at that time was considered to be quite rude:

> I passed by your window
> When you were undressed
> You took off your knickers
> And stood in your vest.

When she asked him who taught him it he replied, "Our Mollie." So bang—I had it again.

Mind you, some of the antics we got up to were enough to try the patience of Job, and I often wonder how in the world we got away with some of the outrageous things that we did.

One day about four or five of us village girls were playing in Rainer's backyard. We were having a high old time chasing and hiding in the many outhouses that they had. Lena, the daughter of the house, had a lovely plait of shiny hair, as thick as your arm it was, which hung down her back, whereas mine was chopped off short because I was always catching nits in it. I was chasing her up some old loft steps when I spied a huge pair of gloving shears, I took hold of them and Lena's hair, held her down and cut her lovely thick plait off at the top near her neck.

Needless to say, I was banned from playing in the Rainer's yard after that.

And once my brothers caught Alfred Knowles as he was coming home across the moors. They took his trousers off, tied his hands behind his back and tied a live grass snake round his neck and sent him on his way. His father was absolutely furious and came rushing up to our house to complain. Our step-father, who looked upon the whole thing as a bit of tomfoolery, told him not to make such a namby pamby of the boy. This made Mr Knowles even more furious and he shouted at our step-father saying, "I'll pull your nose as long as a pound of sausages, that's what I'll do, your kids are like a lot of heathens, that's what they are," he cried.

Another thing we got a hiding for was when we went down to Barratt's barn pinching locust beans and black treacle. The farmer used to buy these things to mix up with the cattle feed, and once the word got round that a farmer had got his locust beans and treacle in, then most of the children in the village made a bee-line for the barn at some time or other. Well, we made for the barn, creeping round the side so that the farmer did not see us. We stuffed our coat pockets with the sweet, hard beans and helped ourselves to the thick black treacle, drinking it from an old enamelled mug that we found in the barn. I think we must have had more than our share of the treacle, because we certainly did not need our weekly customary dose of Beecham Pills. We were up and down the garden to the old lavatory of ours for about twenty-four hours. "Serves you right for pinching," our Mother told us.

"I don't like the look of the weather," our Mother remarked one super sunny morning. "That's too bright to last." I could not see a cloud in the china blue sky.

"I remember one of my Dad's expressions of very bright mornings," she went on, "he used to say that it was 'too gay tu hold', and I reckon it's going to be like that today."

"And look at that roof of our old wash-house," she remarked, "half an hour ago that was wet with dew, now it's as dry as a bone, that's another sure sign that it'll rain later on in the day, when the dew disappears quickly. Never mind," she prattled on, "I promised to take you all out today, so we'll go, but we shall have to look sharp and get out before the weather changes."

It was only to be one of her wooding jaunts, but goodness knows what else we might come home with, maybe a lost dog, or an injured bird, or a handful of wild duck eggs, and always armfuls of wild flowers.

But just outside our gate we met Bertha Botherum. Botherum was not her proper surname, but a nickname that our step-father had tacked on to her, because all she seemed to do was to "bother" about other folks business. "She's got too much of that the cat licks his backside with," he remarked rudely one day, "always going on about somebody she is."

Bertha was very pale with a thin wisp of hair, and as skinny as a bean pole—too much running from one house to another gossiping is what makes her like that, the village people said. It was true too, she was never still, but for ever chasing about with snippets of gossip.

"Thought you'd like to know, missus," she started. Our Mother tried hard not to listen to her outpourings.

"Oh Bertha," she said, "can't you find anything else to talk about except pregnant girls and dirty old men? Look," she went on, "look at that lovely sky, blue as blue, and you just come and take a peek at my wallflowers—you never see such colours and the smell nearly takes your breath away."

So we all traipsed back into the yard.

"Yes, Kitty," Bertha said, "they be very nice and they smells nicer but did I tell you that Mr Miller been at it again?" Our Mother quickly shushed her, not wanting us to hear.

"It's no good, Bertha," she went on, pushing us out of the yard, "I can't stop jawing to you any longer, I've promised my children a walk and that's where we are going," and we made off down the road at a fair pace leaving Bertha standing there open mouthed. "Talks as her belly guides her," our Mother remarked. "Pity the poor souls got nothing else to do."

Then we met Mrs Ainsbury, she was puffing up to Witney on her bicycle, but jumped off quickly when she saw us. She was fat and round, and had what our step-father termed as "bikerider's buttocks". It was true too—her rear end was as rounded as a cow's backside, but we liked her much better than Bertha.

"Where do you think you are all off to?" she asked.

"Well," our Mother said, "I promised I'd take um for a walk, I thought we could pick up a bit of fire-wood on our way back, but it won't be fine for long I'm afraid, just look at them aspen leaves. When they shows their petticoats like that, 'tis a sure sign that it'll rain before very long." She was right too, a slight breeze had sprung up whipping up the leaves so that only the under-sides were showing.

"I must just tell you about our tom cat," Mrs Ainsbury said. "You knows that lovely big cat of mine Joey. Well, I wanted him doctored you see, so my husband suggested that we should get long Harry from Cote to do it. Well he come last night and done it, but I shouldn't have let him if I'd have knowd. We was sitting in our living-room and in comes long Harry. 'Wur is 'e then?' he asked, and there was my poor Joey a-sleeping on the couch so peaceful like. 'Is this 'im?" he ses, catchin' hold of him. And before you could blink yer eye, he'd got his head stuffed in a sack, with the rest of his body sticking out. 'Yer,' he said to my husband, 'ketch 'old of his neck tight, so he don't get out.' Then he whips out his pocket knife, as sharp as a razor it was, turns the cat's backside towards him and before you could say Jack Robinson he'd cut out the necessary, and then, howling like a banshee that old cat streaked out of the house as if all the dogs in the kingdom was after him. Anyhow he seems all right this morning, long Harry said he would be, but I shouldn't have had it done if I'd have knowd."

"Well, I won't hinder you no longer Kitty," Mrs Ainsbury said, twisting her bicycle pedals round so that she could mount her machine easier, then she puffed off, hardly managing to squeeze herself between the saddle and the handlebars.

"What's a cat's necessary, Mum?" I enquired, as we made our way down the Curbridge Road.

"Never you mind," she replied sharply. "You and Bet hop over that gate and pick some flowers. And don't tread that grass down too much," she called, "old Albert will be cutting that any day now."

We climbed over the rickety wooden gate and stood waist high in the field of moon daisies. I do not think I will ever forget that fleeting wonderful feeling; it was one of those never-to-be-forgotten tranquil moments. The slight breeze blew across the waving grass making it look like a beautiful green and white summer sea, cuckoos called from every direction and the hot morning sun bore down. We seemed to float about that green flecked sea, gathering moon daisies, ragged robins, buttercups, hens and chickens, babies rattles, clover and sorrel, disturbing bright butterflies and bumbling bees.

Our shoes and ankles were yellow with pollen from the buttercups, and our arms were full of those sweet summer flowers.

Then our Mother called us back on to the road again.

"Come on," she cried, "while you two have been mooning about picking them flowers, we have been busy finding all this wood," she said, puffing slightly under her heavy load. Still wearing her big apron, she had gathered up the two bottom corners and filled it with chunky bits of wood. The rest of the family had a few sticks in their arms too.

"We had best make tracks for home straight away," she cried, "them rain clouds are coming up fast from the west, come on, best foot forward," she shouted, and striking up with "It's a long way to Tipperary" she led off down the road. We made our way behind her, straggling along, each carrying our treasures. We must have looked like a drawing of ancient Egyptians, bearing gifts to a Pharaoh.

It was a moment to be savoured, to be gently stowed away at the back of the mind, so that it could be brought out again, looked at and dusted, and stowed back again.

The next year Betty left school and went off to service, to work as a kitchen-maid in a big house miles away. For the rest of us the next few years were spent laughing and crying, playing and working, noisily and clumsily the days of our childhood sped by. Soon for us all those green growing-up years had gone for ever.